Passwords
Social Studies Vocabulary
World Geography and Cultures

Curriculum Associates

To the Student

What is a **tsunami**? What is the difference between **latitude** and **longitude**? Where can you find a **coral reef**? *Passwords: Social Studies Vocabulary* will help you learn the words you need to do well in social studies. The lessons in this book are about social studies you will be studying.

Every lesson focuses on ten words that will help you understand the topic. The lessons include a reading selection that uses all ten vocabulary words. Four practice activities follow the reading selection. Using each vocabulary word many times will help you remember the word and its meaning. A writing activity ends the lesson. You will use the vocabulary words you have learned to write a comparison, an informational article, a description, or an opinion piece.

If you need help with a vocabulary word as you do the activities, use the Glossary at the back of the book. The Glossary defines each word and shows you the correct way to pronounce the word. It also has pictures to help you understand the meaning of difficult words.

As you work on the lessons, you may learn other social studies words besides the vocabulary words. Keep track of those other words in My Social Studies Vocabulary on pages 94–98.

Turn to pages 99 and 100 to learn about roots, prefixes, and suffixes. Find out how they can help you understand social studies words.

ISBN 978-0-7609-4495-0
©2008—Curriculum Associates, LLC
North Billerica, MA 01862
No part of this book may be reproduced by any means
without written permission from the publisher.
All Rights Reserved. Printed in USA.
15 14 13 12 11 10 9 8 7

Table of Contents

Lesson 1:   Geography—Looking at the World 4

Lesson 2:   The Tools of Geography 10

Lesson 3:   World Cultures 16

Lesson 4:   The United States and Canada 22

Lesson 5:   Latin America 28

Lesson 6:   Europe 34

Lesson 7:   Russia 40

Lesson 8:   North Africa and Southwest Asia 46

Lesson 9:   Africa South of the Sahara 52

Lesson 10:   Central Asia 58

Lesson 11:   South Asia 64

Lesson 12:   Southeast Asia 70

Lesson 13:   East Asia 76

Lesson 14:   China 82

Lesson 15:   Oceania, Australia, and Antarctica 88

My Social Studies Vocabulary 94

Root Words 99

Prefixes and Suffixes 100

Glossary 101

LESSON 1

geography	climate	agriculture	delta	civilization
landform	vegetation	fertile	river system	irrigation

What is the relationship between land and people? Read this selection to learn how land and people are linked.

Geography—Looking at the World

Geography and Geographers

Geography is the study of the earth and the relationship between people and the earth. Landforms are part of geography. A **landform** is a feature of Earth's surface. Mountains and valleys are landforms.

Weather is an important part of life on Earth. **Climate** is the weather in an area over a period of time. There are several different kinds of climate. Climate shapes what kind of vegetation is in an area. **Vegetation** is the plants in an area. It includes trees, bushes, and grasses. Climate also affects how many people live in an area.

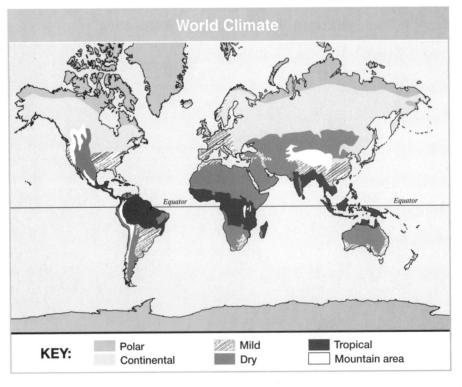

World Climate

KEY:
- Polar
- Continental
- Mild
- Dry
- Tropical
- Mountain area

Equator

Geographers study geography. They ask how land, people, and plants affect one another. For example, more people live in valleys than on top of mountains. Why? Valleys are warmer. They have lakes and rivers. People, plants, and animals need water to live.

Landforms That Attract Settlers

Early people settled on flat land. They could grow crops there. Growing crops is called **agriculture**. It began about 10,000 years ago. Early farmers learned that crops grew well in certain places. Land that is **fertile** is able to produce many crops.

Land in river deltas is fertile. A **delta** is low, watery land. It is formed by a fan-shaped system of streams near the mouth of a river.

Why is a delta fertile? Rich soil is carried downstream by a river system. A **river system** is a network of streams and rivers. It feeds into the main river.

Rivers begin as many fast-flowing streams. Then, they join a river. Near the river's mouth, the river flows more slowly. The river carries mud. The mud builds up. It becomes the richest farmland.

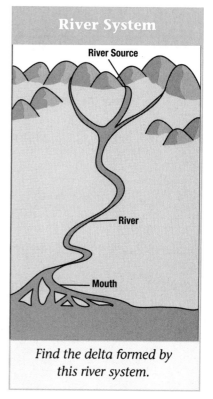

River System

River Source

River

Mouth

Find the delta formed by this river system.

Where Civilizations Form

A **civilization** is a large, organized, group of people. Many civilizations spring up along rivers. Farmers learned that they could use river water for irrigation. **Irrigation** is the process of bringing water to dry land.

Rivers also let people travel from one place to another. People began to trade goods with one another. Even today, many cities are located near sources of water. Where there is water, there is life.

Irrigation helps modern farmers grow more crops.

My Social Studies Vocabulary

Go to page 94 to list other words you have learned about geography.

geography   climate   agriculture   delta   civilization

landform   vegetation   fertile   river system   irrigation

A. *Match each word with its meaning. Write the letter of the correct meaning on the line in front of each word.*

1. _____ river system

2. _____ civilization

3. _____ climate

4. _____ landform

5. _____ irrigation

6. _____ vegetation

7. _____ delta

8. _____ geography

9. _____ agriculture

10. _____ fertile

a. plant life, including trees, bushes, and grasses

b. the process of bringing water to dry land

c. low, watery land formed by a fan-shaped system of streams near the mouth of a river

d. a network of streams and rivers that feed into a main river

e. the study of the earth and the relationship between people and the earth

f. a large, organized, group of people

g. able to produce many crops

h. a feature of Earth's surface

i. the growing of crops

j. the weather in an area over a period of time

geography   climate   agriculture   delta   civilization
landform   vegetation   fertile   river system   irrigation

B. *Circle the word that makes sense in each sentence. Then write the word.*

1. The grasses, bushes, and trees in an area are its (irrigation, vegetation).
   _____

2. Good soil and water are important to (climate, agriculture).
   _____

3. When a river splits into many streams near the mouth of a river,
   a (delta, civilization) is formed. _____

4. A mountain is one kind of (landform, climate). _____

5. Where soil is (delta, fertile), crops grow best. _____

6. People who study the land and the way people use it study
   (geography, civilization). _____

7. There are both streams and rivers in a (river system, landform).
   _____

8. The weather that an area gets over time is its (civilization, climate).
   _____

9. Where the weather and soil are good, a (civilization, landform) might develop.
   _____

10. Water can be brought to dry land by using (agriculture, irrigation).
    _____

WORD ROOT

The word **geography** comes from the Greek
word **geographia**, which means "description
of the earth."

| geography | climate | agriculture | delta | civilization |
| landform | vegetation | fertile | river system | irrigation |

C. *Choose the correct vocabulary word to complete each sentence.*

1. The rich soil near a river's mouth in a _____ is good for growing crops.

2. Good weather, rich soil, and water are a must for _____ .

3. Even if crops do not get enough rain, a farmer could use _____ to water them.

4. When there is much rain in an area, there will be more wild _____ .

5. Land, people, plants, and weather are all part of the study of _____ .

6. A feature of Earth's surface, such as a hill or a valley, is a _____ .

7. The Nile River gave rise to an advanced _____ .

8. A place's weather over time, or its _____ , affects the vegetation that grows there.

9. Water flows from streams and rivers in a _____ .

10. Farmers want to grow crops on land that is _____ .

| geography | climate | agriculture | delta | civilization |
| landform | vegetation | fertile | river system | irrigation |

D. *Use each word in a sentence that shows you understand the meaning of each word.*

1. agriculture _____

   _____

2. irrigation _____

   _____

3. vegetation _____

   _____

4. civilization _____

   _____

5. geography _____

   _____

6. river system _____

   _____

7. climate _____

   _____

8. landform _____

   _____

9. delta _____

   _____

10. fertile _____

   _____

Write! _____

Write your response to the prompt on a separate sheet of paper.
Use as many vocabulary words as you can in your writing.

Geography can affect where and how people live. How do climate and
landforms affect people?

continent   hemisphere   longitude   absolute location   map key

equator   latitude   degree   relative location   map scale

How do you find a place where you have never been? Read this selection to find out how geographers describe the location of places.

The Tools of Geography

Maps and Globes

Maps and globes show Earth. A map is a flat view of all—or part—of Earth. A globe is a round model of Earth. It shows all of Earth's oceans, large bodies of salt water. It also shows continents. A **continent** is one of Earth's seven major landmasses. The continent we live on is North America.

The **equator** is an imaginary line. It runs around the middle of Earth. It divides Earth into two hemispheres. A **hemisphere** is half of Earth. The Northern Hemisphere is north of the equator. The Southern Hemisphere is south of the equator.

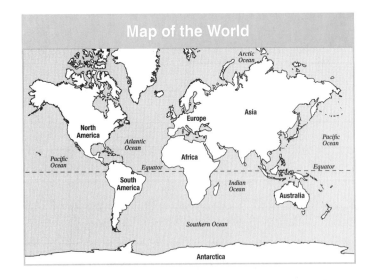

Map of the World

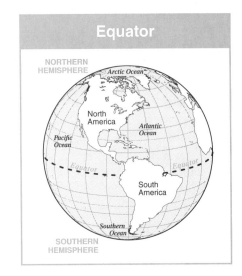

Equator

Latitude and Longitude

Other imaginary lines further divide Earth. **Latitude** is a series of imaginary lines that circle Earth from east to west. **Longitude** is a series of imaginary lines that run from the North Pole to the South Pole.

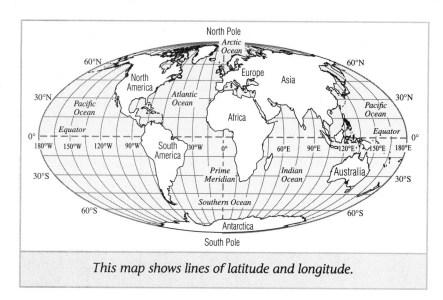

This map shows lines of latitude and longitude.

Latitude and longitude are measured in degrees. A **degree** is one 360th of the distance around Earth. Degrees are shown by this symbol: °. Each degree can be further divided into 60 minutes ('). Each minute can be further divided into 60 seconds (").

Latitude is measured north and south of the equator. The equator is 0°. Longitude is measured from a starting point of 0° called the prime meridian. **Absolute location** is a place's exact location on a grid of latitude and longitude. For example, the absolute location of the White House is 38°53'52"N × 77°2'15"W. That means *38 degrees, 53 minutes, 52 seconds north latitude, 77 degrees, 2 minutes, 15 seconds west longitude.* **Relative location** is the position of one place in relation to another place. For example, *California is south of Oregon.*

Map Parts

Many maps have a key. A **map key** tells what the lines, colors, and symbols on a map mean.

A map key may also have a scale. A **map scale** compares the distance shown on a map to real distances on Earth. For example, 1 inch on a map might be 500 miles on Earth. The map scale would show this as *1 inch = 500 miles.*

> **My World Geography Vocabulary**
> Go to page 94 to list other words you have learned about the tools of geography.

continent	hemisphere	longitude	absolute location	map key
equator	latitude	degree	relative location	map scale

A. *Fill in the blanks with the correct vocabulary word.*

1. the position of one place in relation to another place

   — — — — — — — —   — — — — — — — —

2. a unit that measures latitude and longitude

   — — — — — —

3. a half of Earth

   — — — — — — — — — —

4. imaginary lines that circle Earth from east to west

   — — — — — — — —

5. an imaginary line around the middle of Earth

   — — — — — — —

6. a comparison between the distance shown on a map and actual distances on Earth

   — — —   — — — — —

7. imaginary lines that run from the North Pole to the South Pole

   — — — — — — — — —

8. one of Earth's seven major landmasses

   — — — — — — — — —

9. it tells what the lines, colors, and symbols on a map mean

   — — —   — — —

10. a place's exact location on a grid of latitude and longitude

    — — — — — — — —   — — — — — — — —

continent	hemisphere	longitude	absolute location	map key
equator	latitude	degree	relative location	map scale

B. *Choose and write the two words that best complete each sentence.*

hemisphere	longitude	relative location	continent

1. In which _____ can you find the

   _____ of North America?

degree	map scale	equator	relative location

2. The _____ measurement of latitude at the

   _____ is 0.

equator	map key	map scale	absolute location

3. To understand distance on a map, look at a map's _____ ;

   to understand what map colors mean, look at the _____ .

degree	map	relative location	absolute location

4. Describe a place's _____ by giving its latitude and

   longitude, or give its _____ by telling what it is near.

map scale	latitude	longitude	equator

5. On a map, the lines of _____ go from north to south, and

   the lines of _____ go from east to west.

ROOT

The root of the word **equator** is the Latin word **aequare**, which means "make equal."

continent	hemisphere	longitude	absolute location	map key
equator	latitude	degree	relative location	map scale

C. *Choose the correct vocabulary word to complete each sentence.*

1. To find out how far north a place is, look at its _____ .

2. The units of measure of latitude and longitude are the _____ , minute, and second.

3. The location of Adelaide, Australia, at 34°55'S × 138°36'E, is an _____ .

4. Each of Earth's seven largest land masses is a _____ .

5. If you describe Iraq as being between Iran and Saudi Arabia, you are giving Iraq's _____ .

6. A word for "half of Earth" is _____ .

7. To find the distance between two cities on a map, look at the _____ .

8. A globe shows the _____ as being halfway between the North and South Poles.

9. To understand what colors on a map mean, look at the _____ .

10. Lines of _____ run from the North Pole to the South Pole.

The Tools of Geography

| continent | hemisphere | longitude | absolute location | map key |
| equator | latitude | degree | relative location | map scale |

D. *Use each word in a sentence that shows you understand the meaning of the word.*

1. latitude _____

_____

2. equator _____

_____

3. continent _____

_____

4. map scale _____

_____

5. absolute location _____

_____

6. map key _____

_____

7. degree _____

_____

8. longitude _____

_____

9. relative location _____

_____

10. hemisphere _____

_____

Write! _____

Write your response to the prompt on a separate sheet of paper.
Use as many vocabulary words as you can in your writing.

Suppose that a being from another world asked you how people find things on Earth. What would you say?

culture   economy   urban   population density

culture region   migration   industrialization   cultural diversity

government   rural

What would your life be like if you lived in another place? In this passage, you'll read about how people in different places are alike and different.

World Cultures

Describing a Culture

Every community has a culture. **Culture** is the way of life of a group of people. People in a culture usually have the same religion, customs, laws, music, and art. A **culture region** is an area where many people share the same culture.

Cattle are central to the life of the Maasai.

Land shapes a people's culture. In East Africa, the climate is hot and dry. The land is flat grassland with few trees. Homes of the Maasai are built of mud, not wood. Families own cattle. The cattle graze on the grassland.

Government and Economy

Cultures are influenced by a government. A **government** is a small group of people who make laws to rule a large group of people.

Cultures are also influenced by the economy of a country or region. An **economy** is a system in which people sell or trade goods and services. A strong economy depends on having goods to buy and people with money.

Governments and economies are different from place to place. Both affect what people's lives will be like.

Cultures change when people move. **Migration** is the movement of people from one place to another. They can move from one country to another. They can move within a country.

At one time, most of the world's people lived in rural areas. A **rural** area has many open spaces and few people. Many people in rural areas are farmers.

Now, more people live in **urban**, or city, areas. People move to urban areas for work. **Industrialization** is the making of many goods by machine. It creates many jobs. So, the population density is greater in urban areas. **Population density** is the average number of people per square mile living in an area.

This urban area has a high population density.

This desert region has a low population density.

People from many different cultures often move into the same area. Such an area with people from many cultures has **cultural diversity**.

My World Geography Vocabulary

Go to page 94 to list other words you have learned about world cultures.

culture	economy	urban	population density
culture region	migration	industrialization	cultural diversity
government	rural		

A. *Fill in the blanks with the correct vocabulary word.*

1. a system in which people sell or trade goods and services

    — — — — — — —

2. the movement of people from one place to another

    — — — — — — — — —

3. related to the city

    — — — — —

4. an area where many people share the same culture

    — — — — — — —   — — — — — —

5. the making of many goods by machine

    — — — — — — — — — — — — — — — — —

6. the state that results from having many cultures in the same area

    — — — — — — — —   — — — — — — — — —

7. the way of life of a group of people

    — — — — — — —

8. the average number of people per square mile living in an area

    — — — — — — — — — —   — — — — — — —

9. related to open space or countryside

    — — — — —

10. a small group of people who make laws and rule a large group of
    people

    — — — — — — — — — —

culture	economy	urban	population density
culture region	migration	industrialization	cultural diversity
government	rural		

B. *Circle the word that makes sense in each sentence. Then write the word.*

1. What businesses offer and what people buy creates an (industrialization, economy). _____

2. People follow laws made by their (culture region, government).
   _____

3. Getting a better job is one reason for people's (urban, migration) to cities.
   _____

4. There are many people living closely together in (urban, rural) areas.
   _____

5. When people in an area share the same language, religion, laws, and customs, they are in a (culture region, migration). _____

6. When an area has (cultural diversity, population density), people from many cultures live there. _____

7. Cities have a greater (population density, government) than rural areas have.
   _____

8. Cities often grow as a result of (culture, industrialization).
   _____

9. People who have the same way of life have the same (cultural diversity, culture).
   _____

10. Almost all farmers live in (rural, economy) areas. _____

WORD ROOT

The word **culture** comes from the Latin word **cultus**, which means "care for" or "tend."

culture	economy	urban	population density
culture region	migration	industrialization	cultural diversity
government	rural		

C. *Choose the correct vocabulary word to complete each pair of sentences.*

1. A city with people from 50 countries has _____ .
   Many languages are spoken in an area with _____ .

2. That area is a _____ because its people all have the same culture.
   North Africa is a _____ because its people have the same background.

3. A group's language, religion, and customs are part of its
   _____ .
   A group of people's way of life is their _____ .

4. A farm would be in a _____ area.
   You would not find any cities in a _____ area.

5. The number of people in an area is its _____ .
   A city has a high _____ .

6. Factories and jobs were created by the rise of _____ .
   People moved to city areas because of _____ .

7. The opposite of *rural* is _____ .
   Cities are _____ areas.

8. When people have good jobs and money to spend, the
   _____ is strong.
   The buying and selling of goods and services make up a place's
   _____ .

9. Jobs in cities created a _____ to cities from farms.
   To get away from war is a reason for _____ .

10. A group's laws are made by its _____ .
    A culture is influenced by its _____ .

culture	economy	urban	population density
culture region	migration	industrialization	cultural diversity
government	rural		

D. *Use each pair of words in a sentence.*

1. culture region, cultural diversity

   _____

   _____

   _____

2. culture, government

   _____

   _____

   _____

3. urban, population density

   _____

   _____

   _____

4. industrialization, migration

   _____

   _____

   _____

5. rural, economy

   _____

   _____

   _____

Write! _____

**Write your response to the prompt on a separate sheet of paper.
Use as many vocabulary words as you can in your writing.**

How might two people from different cultures be alike and different?

natural resource   plain   capitalism   technology

mountain range   standard of living   market economy   free trade

tributary   immigrant

How much do you know about the country you live in? What do you know about neighboring countries? Read this selection to learn about the land and people of the United States and Canada.

The United States and Canada

A Richness of Natural Resources

The United States and Canada are rich nations. Much of their wealth comes from having many natural resources. A **natural resource** is something in nature that people can use. It can be water, soil, trees, minerals, or oil.

Both countries get some of their water from rain and melted snow that drains from mountain ranges. A **mountain range** is a long chain of mountains. When water reaches the land below the mountains, it forms tributaries. A **tributary** is a stream that joins others and flows into a river or lake. These waterways provide water to drink and to water crops.

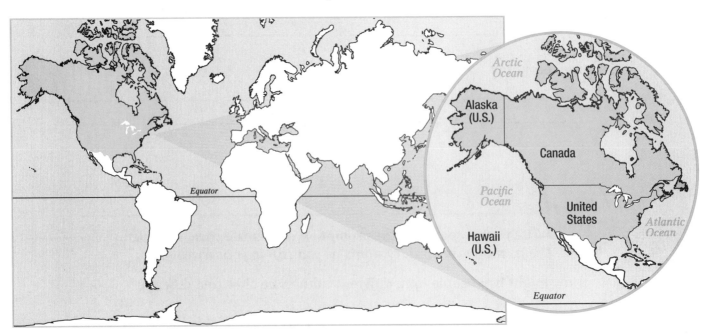

Both countries also have vast plains. A **plain**, also called a prairie, is a flat land with few trees. The Great Plains in the United States and the Interior Plains in Canada have fertile soil.

The western area of both countries is rich in forests. They supply wood for building. Both countries also have minerals, such as copper and iron, and oil.

The United States and Canada Today

Both the United States and Canada have a high standard of living. A **standard of living** is a measure of the quality of life. A high standard of living includes having good food, housing, education, and healthcare. The high standard of living attracts many immigrants. An **immigrant** is someone who comes to a country to live.

The high standard of living is due to three reasons. First, both countries have many natural resources. Second, both have stable governments. Third, both governments favor capitalism. In **capitalism**, private owners control and use resources for profit.

Capitalism creates a **market economy**. Business owners compete with one another to sell goods and services. Capitalism also encourages a growth in technology. **Technology** is the use of new ideas and machines to improve people's lives. Common technologies are automotive, medical, and computers.

The United States and Canada work together to make their economies stronger. They now have a free trade agreement. **Free trade** is the selling of goods from one country to another without taxes. This has made goods cheaper to buy.

Leaders from the United States, Canada, and Mexico sign a free trade agreement.

Mineral Deposits in the United States and Canada

KEY:		
⚒ Oil	◆ Coal	
⊓ Uranium	▲ Lead & Zinc	✪ Copper
✳ Silver	◪ Iron	◇ Gold

My World Geography Vocabulary

Go to page 95 to list other words you have learned about the United States and Canada.

The United States and Canada

natural resource	plain	capitalism	technology
mountain range	standard of living	market economy	free trade
tributary	immigrant		

A. *Match each word with its meaning. Write the letter of the correct meaning on the line in front of each word.*

1. ____ standard of living

2. ____ market economy

3. ____ free trade

4. ____ mountain range

5. ____ natural resource

6. ____ capitalism

7. ____ technology

8. ____ tributary

9. ____ immigrant

10. ____ plain

a. a flat land with few trees

b. the use of new ideas and machines to improve people's lives

c. a stream that joins others and flows into a river or lake

d. someone who comes to a country to live

e. a system in which business owners compete with one another to sell goods and services

f. an economic system in which private owners control and use resources for profit

g. a long chain of mountains

h. the selling of goods from one country to another without taxes

i. something in nature that people can use

j. a measure of the quality of life

The United States and Canada

natural resource	plain	capitalism	technology
mountain range	standard of living	market economy	free trade
tributary	immigrant		

B.   *Circle the word that makes sense in each sentence. Then write the word.*

1.   People might grow crops on a (mountain range, plain) because the soil is
      fertile. _____

2.   A person who moves from Canada to France to live is an
      (standard of living, immigrant) . _____

3.   When rain drains from a mountain range, it might form a stream that
      becomes a (tributary, natural resource) to a river. _____

4.   When people have everything they need to have a good life, they have a high
      (capitalism, standard of living). _____

5.   When businesses compete to sell goods and services, that creates a
      (market economy, immigrant). _____

6.   A mineral is a (natural resource, technology). _____

7.   Americans who buy Canada's goods will pay less than they once did because of
      a (free trade, market economy) agreement. _____

8.   The Rocky Mountains are a (mountain range, tributary) in the United States
      and Canada. _____

9.   Business owners in the United States and Canada can decide what to make and sell
      because their countries believe in (free trade, capitalism). _____

10. American and Canadian citizens have many new kinds of products because of
      (plain, technology). _____

ROOT

The word **plain** comes from the Latin word
planus, which means "flat."

natural resource	plain	capitalism	technology
mountain range	standard of living	market economy	free trade
tributary	immigrant		

C. *Choose the correct vocabulary word to complete each sentence.*

1. If a government encourages _____ , some people will start a business.

2. Businesses compete with one another in a _____ .

3. People in the United States and Canada can buy each other's products without taxes because of a _____ agreement.

4. People have a wide variety of new products because of _____ .

5. Oil is an important _____ in the United States and Canada.

6. In the United States or Canada, an _____ might meet many other people from the country from which she moved.

7. People who are poor, have little food, and live in shacks have a low _____ .

8. One source of water is melted snow from a _____ .

9. Another name for a prairie is a _____ .

10. Water flows into a river or lake from a _____ .

natural resource	plain	capitalism	technology
mountain range	standard of living	market economy	free trade
tributary	immigrant		

D. *Use each word in a sentence that shows you understand the meaning of the word.*

1. tributary _____

   _____

2. immigrant _____

   _____

3. capitalism _____

   _____

4. plain _____

   _____

5. mountain range _____

   _____

6. market economy _____

   _____

7. standard of living _____

   _____

8. free trade _____

   _____

9. natural resource _____

   _____

10. technology _____

   _____

Write!

Write your response to the prompt on a separate sheet of paper.
Use as many vocabulary words as you can in your writing.

What are some things the United States and Canada have in common?

volcano	tropical climate	developing country	export
elevation	colonization	cash crop	deforestation
plateau	descendant		

Latin America includes Mexico, Central America, the Caribbean, and South America. It is called "Latin" America because the languages that are spoken there, Spanish and Portuguese, have their roots in Latin.

Latin America

Lands of Great Variety

Latin America has amazing landforms! For instance, Mexico and Central America have volcanoes. A **volcano** is an opening in Earth's crust through which liquid rock and gases flow.

The Andes Mountains are amazing too. They are among the highest mountains in the world. The **elevation**, or height, of some mountains reaches almost 23,000 feet.

A vast **plateau**, a high, flat landform, covers much of central Mexico. The soil is very rich. But the area gets little rain.

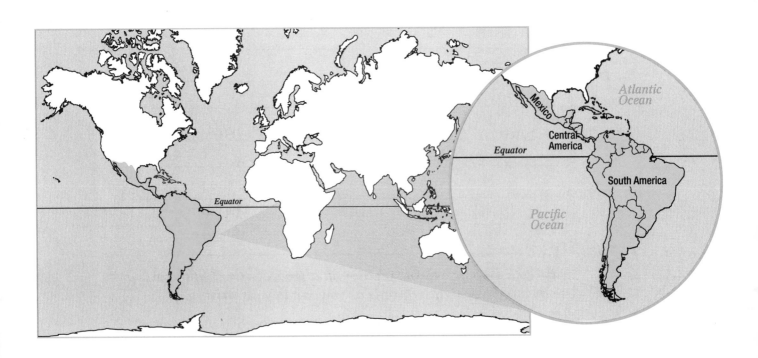

Much of Latin America has a tropical climate. A **tropical climate** is always very warm and moist. Parts of Central and South America have tropical rain forests. These are lush, dense forests. They get as much as 260 inches of rain per year! The rain creates vast rivers. One is the Amazon in Brazil.

A Spanish-Portuguese Past

Once, only Native Americans lived in Latin America. In the 1500s, people from Spain and Portugal began to build settlements. This was the beginning of **colonization**. The Spanish and Portuguese brought African slaves to Latin America. Now, many Latin Americans are descendants of Native Americans, early settlers, and former slaves. A **descendant** is someone related to an earlier person or group.

The effect of these early settlers remains today. Most people speak Spanish. In Brazil, Portuguese is a common language. Also, most people are Catholic, a Christian religion. It was the religion of the early settlers.

Catholic churches can be found in almost every city and town in Latin America.

Latin America Today

Many countries have a low standard of living. Their people have no electricity or running water. Harsh military leaders run some countries. Poorer countries are called developing countries. A **developing country** is moving from an economy based on farming to one based on industry.

Most countries try to increase their wealth by selling cash crops for export. A **cash crop** is a crop that is raised to sell. An **export** is a good that is sold to another country. Cash crops include coffee, bananas, pineapples, and sugar cane.

Farmers cut down tropical forests to grow cash crops. But **deforestation**, the cutting down of forests, also kills many plants and animals.

Deforestation has reduced the size of the tropical forest.

Some countries, such as Costa Rica, are stopping deforestation. Why? Because people will travel there to see the plants and animals in tropical forests. They bring in more money than growing cash crops in deforested areas!

My World Geography Vocabulary

Go to page 95 to list other words you have learned about Latin America.

volcano	tropical climate	developing country	export
elevation	colonization	cash crop	deforestation
plateau	descendant		

A. *Match each word with its meaning. Write the letter of the correct meaning on the line in front of each word.*

1. _____ developing country

2. _____ tropical climate

3. _____ deforestation

4. _____ colonization

5. _____ descendant

6. _____ cash crop

7. _____ volcano

8. _____ plateau

9. _____ export

10. _____ elevation

a. a crop that is raised to sell

b. someone related to an earlier person or group

c. a country that is moving from an economy based on farming to one based on industry

d. height, as in the measure of mountains

e. a good that is sold to another country

f. a high, flat landform

g. weather that is always very warm and moist

h. the setting up of settlements in another country

i. the cutting down of forests

j. an opening in Earth's crust through which rock and gases flow

volcano	tropical climate	developing country	export
elevation	colonization	cash crop	deforestation
plateau	descendant		

B. *Choose and write the two words that best complete each sentence.*

| plateau | tropical climate | volcano | export |

1. In Mexico, you might see a _____ spewing liquid rock

   or a high, flat _____ .

| deforestation | elevation | tropical climate | plateau |

2. Rain forests are found in areas with a _____ where the

   _____ is usually low.

| volcano | export | colonization | cash crop |

3. Coffee can be grown as a _____ and then sold as an

   _____ to other countries.

| deforestation | elevation | descendant | developing country |

4. Stopping _____ might make a _____

   richer.

| descendant | developing country | colonization | cash crop |

5. A Native American is not the _____ of

   a Spanish settler involved in the _____ of the region.

ROOT

The root of **export** is the Latin word **portare**,
which means "carry."

Latin America

31

volcano	tropical climate	developing country	export
elevation	colonization	cash crop	deforestation
plateau	descendant		

C. *Choose the correct vocabulary word to complete each pair of sentences.*

1. Land that is high and flat is a _____ .

   Central Mexico has a large, flat _____ .

2. Sugar grown for sale is a _____ .

   A farmer sells a _____ instead of eating it.

3. The climate in Central America is a _____ .

   People who like heat and rain like Central America's

   _____ .

4. The Spanish and Portuguese led the _____ of Latin

   America.

   Making a settlement is the first step in _____ .

5. An opening in Earth's crust through which liquid rock can pour is a

   _____ .

   In Mexico, you might see a _____ spilling out liquid rock.

6. A person who is a _____ of Spanish people may speak

   Spanish, too.

   A Latin American is probably a _____ of one of three

   early groups.

7. A country that is moving from agriculture to industry is a _____ .

   Peru is a _____ in Latin America.

8. The United States might buy an _____ from Latin America.

   Countries can get richer by selling a crop as an _____ .

9. A mountain with a high _____ may have snow on top.

   A plain has a low _____ .

10. Plants and animals die when _____ happens.

    Where there is _____ , the land is bare.

 32

volcano	tropical climate	developing country	export
elevation	colonization	cash crop	deforestation
plateau	descendant		

D. *Use each word in a sentence that shows you understand the meaning of the word.*

1. cash crop _____
_____

2. colonization _____
_____

3. deforestation _____
_____

4. developing country _____
_____

5. elevation _____
_____

6. export _____
_____

7. descendant _____
_____

8. plateau _____
_____

9. tropical climate _____
_____

10. volcano _____
_____

 *Write!* _____

Write your response to the prompt on a separate sheet of paper.
Use as many vocabulary words as you can in your writing.

Would you like to visit Latin America? Why or why not?

peninsula	ethnic conflict	service industry	European Union
channel	border	tourism	common currency
ethnic group	manufacturing		

Europe includes more than 40 countries and 150 ethnic groups. Read this selection to learn how European countries are working together.

Europe

Lots of Water

Water is in and around Europe. Three large peninsulas form a large part of Europe. A **peninsula** is an area of land that is mostly surrounded by water. It is joined to a larger area of land. Inland waterways provide transportation routes throughout Europe.

Not all of Europe is joined, however. Islands are part of Europe, too. For example, a channel separates Great Britain from the main part of Europe. A **channel** is a narrow sea. It runs between two large areas of land.

Europe has many different climates. The Alps are capped with snow all year. The British Isles are cool and rainy. The Mediterranean area is sunny, warm, and dry.

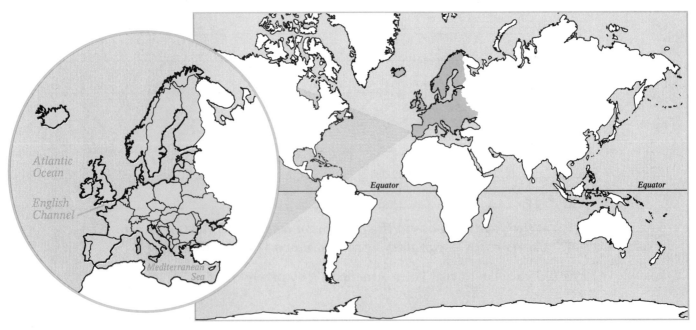

Many Ethnic Groups

Nearly one-eighth of the world's people live in Europe. Each country is home to one or more ethnic groups. An **ethnic group** is a group of people who have common ancestors, history, language, and way of life.

In the past, Europe saw much **ethnic conflict**, or fighting among ethnic groups. Sometimes after a war, the border between countries changed. A **border** is an imaginary line that separates countries.

Europe Today

Europe today is a mix of old and new. Centuries-old buildings stand next to new factories.

Many countries have a high degree of industrialization. **Manufacturing**, the making of goods by machine, is common in most countries. Farming is still important, too. For example, France grows a lot of wheat.

Castles built long ago are found all across Europe.

The service industry is also important. A **service industry** is a group of businesses that provides services. One important service industry is **tourism**. That is the business of helping people travel on vacations. People from all over the world enjoy Europe's fine food, art, and natural beauty.

Many of Europe's countries have formed the **European Union (EU)**. It is a group of countries working together to make better lives for their people.

Chemical manufacturing takes place at this modern European factory.

In 2002, the European Union decided to create a **common currency**. This is a system of money that is shared by different countries. Each country agreed to have the euro as its money. Fewer than 100 years ago, this would have been unthinkable. Then, these countries were at war with one another!

My World Geography Vocabulary

Go to page 96 to list other words you have learned about Europe.

peninsula   ethnic conflict   service industry   European Union
channel   border   tourism   common currency
ethnic group   manufacturing

A.   *Fill in the blanks with the correct vocabulary word.*

1.   a group of businesses that provides services

   __ __ __ __ __ __ __   __ __ __ __ __ __ __ __

2.   an imaginary line that separates countries

   __ __ __ __ __ __

3.   the business of helping people travel on vacations

   __ __ __ __ __ __ __

4.   the making of goods by machine

   __ __ __ __ __ __ __ __ __ __ __ __ __

5.   an area of land that extends from a landmass and is mostly surrounded
     by water

   __ __ __ __ __ __ __ __ __

6.   a system of money that is shared by different countries

   __ __ __ __ __ __   __ __ __ __ __ __ __ __

7.   a group of countries that are working together to make better lives for
     their people

   __ __ __ __ __ __ __   __ __ __ __ __

8.   a group of people who have common ancestors, history, language, and
     a way of life

   __ __ __ __ __ __   __ __ __ __ __

9.   fighting among ethnic groups

   __ __ __ __ __ __   __ __ __ __ __ __ __

10. a narrow sea between two large areas of land

   __ __ __ __ __ __ __

peninsula	ethnic conflict	service industry	European Union
channel	border	tourism	common currency
ethnic group	manufacturing		

B. *Circle the word that makes sense in each sentence. Then write the word.*

1. People in an (ethnic conflict, ethnic group) have many things in common.
    _____

2. After a war, the (peninsula, border) between two countries might change.
    _____

3. Great Britain is separated from the main area of Europe by a (channel, common currency). _____

4. Goods are produced by the (manufacturing, tourism) industry.
    _____

5. Countries who are members of the (service industry, European Union) are working together toward shared goals. _____

6. A large area of land that is surrounded by water on most sides is a (peninsula, channel). _____

7. People who are on vacation are served by the (manufacturing, tourism) industry.
    _____

8. Money looks the same from country to country when the countries share a (border, common currency). _____

9. No goods are produced in a (service industry, European Union).
    _____

10. When fighting between two groups is based on their ethnic background, that is an (ethnic group, ethnic conflict). _____

WORD **ROOT**

The word **ethnic** comes from the Greek word **ethnos**, which means "people" or "nation."

peninsula	ethnic conflict	service industry	European Union
channel	border	tourism	common currency
ethnic group	manufacturing		

C. *Choose the correct vocabulary word to complete each sentence.*

1. Water surrounds a _____ on three sides.

2. A country's _____ with another country might change after a war.

3. In most European countries, some goods are produced by

   _____ .

4. People who have the same language, history, ancestors, and way of life are often in the same _____ .

5. People who are in a business that does not produce goods are in a

   _____ .

6. Improving people's health, wealth, and safety is the goal of the

   _____ .

7. The euro is the _____ of some European countries.

8. People who want to get from the mainland of Europe to Great Britain must cross a _____ .

9. When two ethnic groups go to war with each other, that's

   _____ .

10. Visitors from other countries are helped by those who work in

    _____ .

peninsula	ethnic conflict	service industry	European Union
channel	border	tourism	common currency
ethnic group	manufacturing		

D. *Use each pair of words in a sentence.*

1. European Union, tourism

   _____

   _____

   _____

2. ethnic group, ethnic conflict

   _____

   _____

   _____

3. border, common currency

   _____

   _____

   _____

4. peninsula, channel

   _____

   _____

   _____

5. manufacturing, service industry

   _____

   _____

   _____

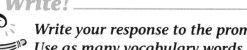

Write! _____

Write your response to the prompt on a separate sheet of paper.
Use as many vocabulary words as you can in your writing.

What do the countries in Europe have in common?

tundra	steppe	collective farm	consumer good
permafrost	communism	privatization	pollution
taiga	command economy		

Russia is a huge country! However, not many people live there.
Read this selection to find out why.

Russia

A Vast, Cold Land

Russia is the world's largest country in area. It stretches across 11 time zones. The Ural Mountains divide European Russia from the main part of Russia.

Much of Russia is cold. In the far north, the climate is subarctic, very cold and frozen. The land here is tundra. A **tundra** is a flat, bare plain with no trees. Snow covers the ground from September through May. A little below the surface, the ground is always frozen. This is called **permafrost**.

South of the tundra is the **taiga**. This is an area of evergreen forests. The ground is not fertile. The climate is cold and windy. There is much snow. South of the taiga are vast steppes. A **steppe** is dry, flat grassland.

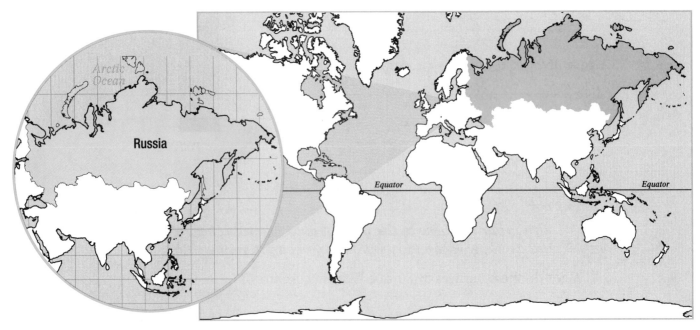

Many Ethnic Groups

There are many different ethnic groups in Russia. They share a history rich in art, music, and books. Also, they have survived the cold climates and many harsh governments.

Russia Today

After 1917, Russia was called the Soviet Union. It took over many formerly free countries. The Soviet form of government was communism. In **communism**, the government owns all property and businesses. The government decides what goods to produce. This is called a **command economy**.

Under communism, Russians often had to stand in line to buy bread.

Every Soviet farm was a **collective farm**. That was a farm that the Soviet government owned and managed. The government gave away the crops as they saw fit. People who worked on collective farms often went hungry.

By the 1980s, communism had failed. People did not want to work when they were not rewarded for it. The government slowly shifted to a democracy, a government by the people. Privatization soon followed. **Privatization** is the process of replacing government ownership of businesses with private ownership. Soon, businesses began to produce consumer goods that people wanted. A **consumer good** is a product that people use. Consumer goods include clothing and automobiles.

The Soviet Union went back to being Russia. It became a democracy. But people's lives did not change quickly. There are often shortages of goods and services. Many people cannot find jobs.

Pollution from factories has harmed Russia.

There is one lasting effect of communism: pollution. **Pollution** is the poisoning of water, land, and air. Careless manufacturing created widespread pollution in Russia.

My World Geography Vocabulary

Go to page 96 to list other words you have learned about Russia.

Russia

tundra   steppe   collective farm   consumer good
permafrost   communism   privatization   pollution
taiga   command economy

A. *Fill in the blanks with the correct vocabulary word.*

1. an area of evergreen forests

   — — — — —

2. an economic system in which the government owns all property and businesses

   — — — — — — — — —

3. the process of replacing government ownership of businesses with private ownership

   — — — — — — — — — — — — —

4. a flat grassland

   — — — — — —

5. a flat, bare plain with no trees

   — — — — — —

6. an economy in which the government decides what goods to produce, not the people or business owners

   — — — — — — —   — — — — — — —

7. a farm that the government owns and manages

   — — — — — — — — — —   — — — —

8. a product that people use

   — — — — — — — —   — — — —

9. the poisoning of water, land, and air

   — — — — — — — — —

10. ground that is always frozen

    — — — — — — — — — —

tundra	steppe	collective farm	consumer good
permafrost	communism	privatization	pollution
taiga	command economy		

B. *Choose and write the two words that best complete each sentence.*

> privatization   communism   command economy   pollution

1. Russian land and water were poisoned by _____ under _____ , the Soviet form of government.

> consumer good   privatization   collective farm   communism

2. After the Russian government allowed the _____ of business, the factory began to produce a new _____ .

> permafrost   taiga   tundra   steppe

3. During summer, the surface of the _____ might be muddy, but a layer of _____ is always frozen under it.

> collective farm   pollution   consumer goods   command economy

4. In a _____ , a factory or _____ produces only what the government tells it to.

> permafrost   taiga   tundra   steppe

5. You would see only grass on a _____ , but there would be trees in an area of _____ .

ROOT

The word **privatization** comes from the Latin word **privus**, meaning "private."

tundra	steppe	collective farm	consumer good
permafrost	communism	privatization	pollution
taiga	command economy		

C. *Choose the correct vocabulary word to complete each sentence.*

1. The cold, windy area of Russia that is covered with forest is the

    _____ .

2. People's needs and wants for goods are not considered in a

    _____ .

3. The part of the ground that is always frozen is _____ .

4. The people who worked on a _____ did not get to keep the

    crops they grew.

5. If you were on a vast grassland in Russia, you would be on a

    _____ .

6. During the days of the Soviet Union, the form of government was

    _____ .

7. After the Soviet Union broke up, the _____ of business led

    to making goods that people wanted.

8. The flat, bare land that is the farthest north in Russia is

    _____ .

9. A television is an example of a _____ .

10. Russia's lakes and rivers continue to suffer from _____ .

tundra   steppe   collective farm   consumer good
permafrost   communism   privatization   pollution
taiga   command economy

D. *Use each word in a sentence that shows you understand the meaning of the word.*

1. taiga _____

_____

2. steppe _____

_____

3. tundra _____

_____

4. pollution _____

_____

5. permafrost _____

_____

6. communism _____

_____

7. privatization _____

_____

8. collective farm _____

_____

9. consumer good _____

_____

10. command economy _____

_____

Write!

*Write your response to the prompt on a separate sheet of paper.
Use as many vocabulary words as you can in your writing.*

What are some challenges that people in Russia have had to face?

North Africa and Southwest Asia (also called the Middle East) have much in common. Read this selection to find out how they are alike.

North Africa and Southwest Asia

Desert Lands

Much of North Africa and Southwest Asia is hot, dry desert. A **desert** is a sandy or rocky area with little or no rainfall. No grass, bushes, or trees grow there. The Sahara, a desert in North Africa, is almost as large as the United States. It does have some areas of greenery, however. An **oasis** is an area in the desert that has water from underground.

Deserts can happen naturally. Or they can be made by people. **Overgrazing** is the practice of allowing animals to graze, or eat, grass faster than it can grow back. All the plants die. Loose soil blows around in the wind. The land then becomes a desert.

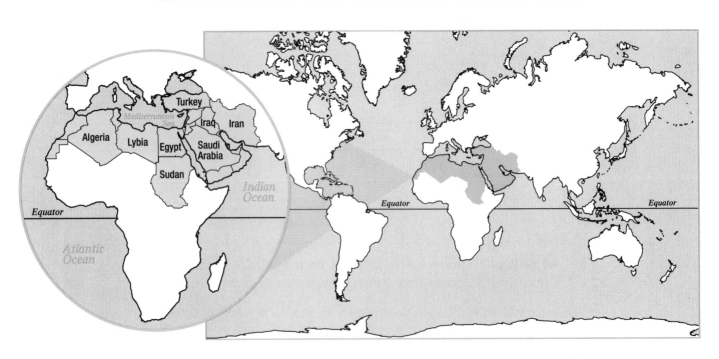

Egypt has the most productive farms in North Africa. But, after overgrazing, less than 5 percent of the land is arable. Land that is **arable** is suitable for use as farmland.

People with a Desert Past

For centuries, various ethnic groups lived in or near the desert. They tended flocks of sheep and herded them from place to place.

More recently, ethnic groups formed countries. Their group loyalty and pride was carried over to the countries in which they live. **Nationalism** is a strong pride in and loyalty to one's nation.

Followers of Islam

Most people here are followers of Islam. **Islam** is a religion based on the teachings of Muhammad. Muhammad taught a belief in one god. Believers in Islam are called Muslims. Muslims pray in a building of worship called a **mosque**.

Muslims worship at a mosque.

Some governments in Muslim countries are theocracies. A **theocracy** is a government ruled by a religious leader.

Riches from Oil

Most countries in North Africa are poor. By contrast, most of Southwest Asia is rich. Countries there have vast fields of petroleum under the ground. **Petroleum** is an oily liquid that people burn to create energy. It is the area's greatest natural resource.

This oil field is in Saudi Arabia.

The world depends on oil as an energy source. The oil supply, the amount available, is limited. The demand, the amount people want, is high. **Supply and demand** is an economic concept. It states that the price of a good rises or falls, depending on how many people want it and on how much of the good is available.

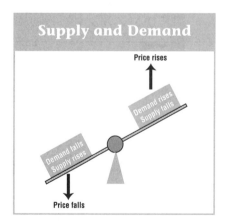

Supply and Demand

Price rises

Demand rises
Supply falls

Demand falls
Supply rises

Price falls

My World Geography Vocabulary

Go to page 96 to list other words you have learned about North Africa and Southwest Asia.

North Africa and Southwest Asia

desert   overgrazing   nationalism   mosque   petroleum

oasis   arable   Islam   theocracy   supply and demand

A. *Match each word with its meaning. Write the letter of the correct meaning on the line in front of each word.*

1. _____ Islam

2. _____ arable

3. _____ mosque

4. _____ nationalism

5. _____ petroleum

6. _____ desert

7. _____ supply and demand

8. _____ overgrazing

9. _____ theocracy

10. _____ oasis

a. what happens when animals eat grass faster than it can grow back

b. suitable for use as farmland

c. a religion based on the teachings of Muhammad

d. a sandy or rocky area with little or no rainfall

e. a government ruled by a religious leader

f. a Muslim building of worship

g. an area in the desert that has water from underground

h. an oily liquid people burn to create energy

i. a strong pride in and loyalty to one's country

j. an economic concept that states that the price of a good rises or falls depending on how many people want it and on how much of the good is available

desert	overgrazing	nationalism	mosque	petroleum
oasis	arable	Islam	theocracy	supply and demand

B. *Choose and write the two words that best complete each sentence.*

Islam	petroleum	theocracy	supply and demand

1. The economic law of _____ helps set the price for

    Southwest Asia's most important natural resource, _____ .

Islam	mosque	nationalism	overgrazing

2. Muslims, people who follow _____ , worship in a special

    place called a _____ .

overgrazing	desert	oasis	arable

3. Crops can grow on land that is _____ , but crop land can

    be lost as a result of _____ by cattle and sheep.

oasis	arable	petroleum	desert

4. Even in a hot, dry _____ like the Sahara, you might see an

    _____ with cool water and some grass.

mosque	supply and demand	nationalism	theocracy

5. People might be united by their _____ , or pride in their

    country, and by being governed in a _____ by a religious

    leader whom they all admire.

WORD ROOT

The word **petroleum** comes from the Latin
words **petra**, which means "rock," and **oleum**,
which means "oil."

| desert | overgrazing | nationalism | mosque | petroleum |
| oasis | arable | Islam | theocracy | supply and demand |

C. *Write the vocabulary word that best completes each pair of sentences.*

1. A farmer can plant a crop on _____ land.

   There is not much _____ land in Southwest Asia.

2. Many people in North Africa are believers in the religion of

   _____ .

   Muslims have _____ as their religion.

3. A religious leader is also the head of government in a _____ .

   You might find a government by _____ in Southwest Asia.

4. Land turns to desert as a result of _____ by sheep.

   Keeping sheep in just one area causes _____ .

5. Southwest Asia's main natural resource is _____ .

   Oil is a word often used to mean _____ .

6. Animals can drink water at an _____ .

   You might find plants growing at an _____ .

7. The availability of and desire for a good is _____ .

   The price of a scarce resource goes up because of _____ .

8. Having pride in one's country is _____ .

   Feelings of _____ are common in Southwest Asia.

9. Muslims pray in a _____ .

   A believer in Islam goes to a _____ .

10. You might describe a _____ as "hot, dry, and sandy."

    There are no trees in a _____ .

North Africa and Southwest Asia

| desert | overgrazing | nationalism | mosque | petroleum |
| oasis | arable | Islam | theocracy | supply and demand |

D. *Use each word in a sentence that shows you understand the meaning of each word.*

1. overgrazing _____
_____

2. Islam _____
_____

3. desert _____
_____

4. mosque _____
_____

5. petroleum _____
_____

6. nationalism _____
_____

7. arable _____
_____

8. supply and demand _____
_____

9. theocracy _____
_____

10. oasis _____
_____

Write! _____

Write your response to the prompt on a separate sheet of paper.
Use as many vocabulary words as you can in your writing.

What makes North Africa and Southwest Asia different from other regions?

drought   rift   overpopulation   life expectancy

savanna   subsistence farming   famine   clan

endangered   illiterate

The land south of the Sahara, the world's largest desert, is called Sub-Saharan Africa. Read this selection to find out about the problems this area faces.

Africa South of the Sahara

Vast Land

Much of Africa is desert or near desert. Deserts can develop naturally. They can be created by **drought**, a long time without rain. But people can also cause deserts to spread, too. Poor farming practices have led to more desert land in this area.

East Africa has a vast savanna. A **savanna** is flat grassland. It has few trees and shrubs. Animals, such as lions and elephants, live on the savanna. Many animals are **endangered**. That means that there are so few of them, they may soon disappear forever. Pollution, development, and farming are destroying the animals' habitats.

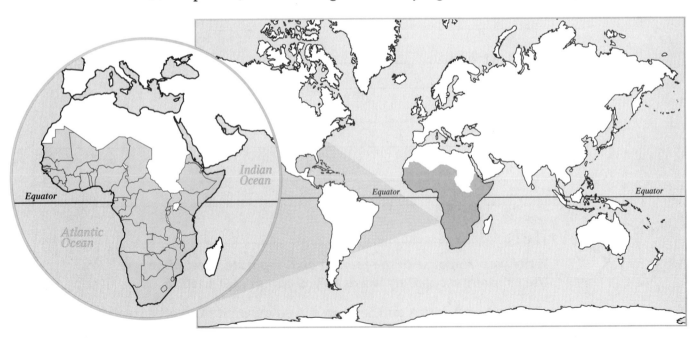

One of Africa's most unusual landforms is the Great Rift Valley. A **rift** is a broad, steep-walled valley. It is a crack in Earth's crust. It is caused by forces beneath the surface. The Great Rift Valley is 4,000 miles long. It is 6,000 feet deep.

Lakes form as parts of the Great Rift Valley fill with water.

Poor People

Most Africans live in villages. Subsistence farming is common. **Subsistence farming** is growing only enough crops to provide for one's basic food needs. Most people are poor. Many are also **illiterate**. This means they are unable to read and write.

Each year, many Africans leave their villages and move to cities. They come looking for jobs and better opportunities. But life in African cities can be hard. Often there is not enough water, power, or housing.

Many Africans have moved away from villages such as this one.

Overpopulation is a problem everywhere. **Overpopulation** is having more people in an area than the resources can support. Some countries have famines. A **famine** is a serious food shortage that causes people to die.

Overpopulation has led to overcrowded cities.

An African's life expectancy is not as long as that for people in other places. **Life expectancy** is how long people are expected to live.

Ethnic Groups and Clans

In all of Africa, there are about 1,000 ethnic groups. In Nigeria, for example, there are more than 200 ethnic groups. Each ethnic group is made up of clans. A **clan** is a group of people who are related.

Many people view their clan as an extended family. Clans provide people with a sense of security and belonging. People are sometimes loyal to their clan first and their country second. This can lead to conflict between clans within a country.

My World Geography Vocabulary

Go to page 96 to list other words you have learned about Africa south of the Sahara.

drought	rift	overpopulation	life expectancy
savanna	subsistence farming	famine	clan
endangered	illiterate		

A. *Fill in the blanks with the correct vocabulary word.*

1. growing only enough crops to provide for one's basic food needs

   __ __ __ __ __ __ __ __ __ __ __   __ __ __ __ __ __ __

2. unable to read and write

   __ __ __ __ __ __ __ __ __ __

3. a long time without rain

   __ __ __ __ __ __ __

4. how long people are expected to live

   __ __ __ __   __ __ __ __ __ __ __ __ __ __

5. a broad, steep-walled valley

   __ __ __ __

6. a serious food shortage that causes people to die

   __ __ __ __ __ __

7. close to disappearing forever because there are so few

   __ __ __ __ __ __ __ __ __ __

8. a group of people who are related

   __ __ __ __

9. flat grassland with a few trees and shrubs

   __ __ __ __ __ __ __

10. having more people in an area than the resources can support

    __ __ __ __ __ __ __ __ __ __ __ __ __ __

drought	rift	overpopulation	life expectancy
savanna	subsistence farming	famine	clan
endangered	illiterate		

B. *Circle the word that makes sense in each sentence. Then write the word.*

1. Africans are often most loyal to their (clan, famine). _____

2. People who can't read are (endangered, illiterate). _____

3. People may go hungry as a result of (overpopulation, life expectancy).

   _____

4. Animals eat grass on a (rift, savanna). _____

5. Forces beneath Earth caused a (rift, drought). _____

6. Crop failure in a large area results in (subsistence farming, famine).

   _____

7. Africans die young and do not have a long (savanna, life expectancy).

   _____

8. Animals that might disappear forever from Earth are (endangered, illiterate).

   _____

9. A lack of rain causes (clan, drought). _____

10. Growing just enough food to live is (subsistence farming, overpopulation).

    _____

WORD ROOT

The word **famine** comes from the Latin word **fames**, meaning "hunger."

drought	rift	overpopulation	life expectancy
savanna	subsistence farming	famine	clan
endangered	illiterate		

C. *Choose the correct vocabulary word to complete each sentence.*

1. If you are in a valley with high, steep sides, you might be in
    a _____ valley.

2. A person who is in a _____ is related to others
    in the group.

3. When people don't have enough to eat and die, the problem is called
    a _____ .

4. Deserts may spread because of overgrazing, poor farming practices,
    or _____ .

5. If an area's resources are not enough for the people living there, the problem
    is called _____ .

6. Elephants live on a _____ , a flat grassland.

7. How long a person is expected to live is his or her
    _____ .

8. Education can help those who are _____ .

9. People who farm and grow just enough food for their own needs
    are practicing _____ .

10. Many kinds of African animals are _____ .

drought	rift	overpopulation	life expectancy
savanna	subsistence farming	famine	clan
endangered	illiterate		

D. *Use each pair of words in a sentence.*

1. famine, overpopulation

   _____

   _____

   _____

2. illiterate, subsistence farming

   _____

   _____

   _____

3. clan, life expectancy

   _____

   _____

   _____

4. rift, savanna

   _____

   _____

   _____

5. endangered, drought

   _____

   _____

   _____

Write! _____

Write your response to the prompt on a separate sheet of paper.
Use as many vocabulary words as you can in your writing.

Describe some of the challenges people in Sub-Saharan Africa face.

landlocked   precipitation   earthquake   nomad   Silk Road
arid   erosion   tribe   tradition   emigrate

*The people of Central Asia have lived in that area for centuries.
Read this selection to learn about them and their land.*

Central Asia

A Dry and Shaken Land

Life in Central Asia is difficult. The area is **landlocked**,
surrounded by land. Much of the land is desert or arid grassland.
Arid means "dry." Other areas get some **precipitation**, water that
falls to Earth as rain or snow. However, when it rains, it rains hard.
Floods from heavy rain cause erosion. **Erosion** is the wearing away of
land by water, wind, or ice.

Earthquakes are common. An **earthquake** is a shaking of part
of Earth's surface as a result of underground forces. Earthquakes can
kill people and cause much damage.

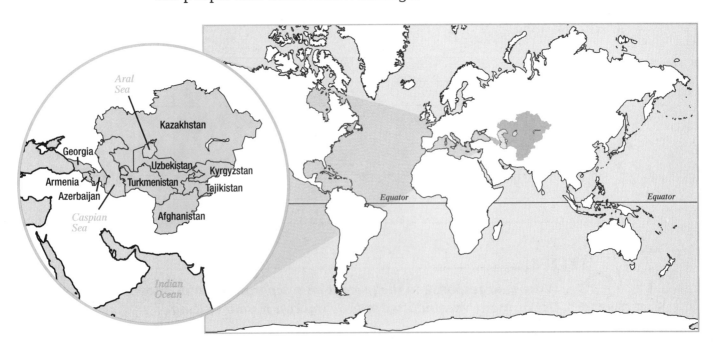

Desert Tribes

Tribes of nomads have lived in this area for centuries. A **tribe** is a group of people who share a way of life. A **nomad** is a person who travels from place to place in search of food or grazing for animals. People in a tribe share a way of life. Each tribe has its own traditions. A **tradition** is a belief or custom handed down from one generation to the next. For instance, many tribes have worn the same styles and colors of clothing for centuries.

This central Asian nomad wears the traditional clothing of his tribe.

The Silk Road

Beginning about 200 B.C., traders took goods from China to markets in Europe. They traveled across Central Asia on the Silk Road. The **Silk Road** was a trade route that went from China, through Central Asia, to the Mediterranean Sea. It took its name from the most popular trade item, silk. By A.D. 1300, the Silk Road was little used. Sea routes had largely replaced overland trade routes.

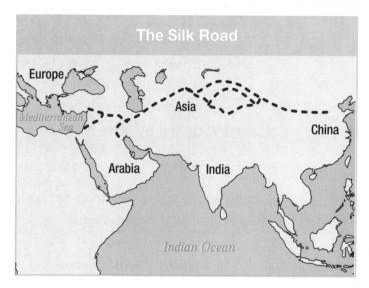

The Silk Road

Europe
Mediterranean Sea
Asia
China
Arabia
India
Indian Ocean

Challenges of the Future

The land in Central Asia is dry. The main sources of water are polluted. The Caspian Sea, the world's largest inland body of water, has poor water quality. Its water has been spoiled by spills from oil drilling and untreated waste from sewers and industry. The Aral Sea is also polluted beyond use.

Young people are emigrating to find better jobs and lives. To **emigrate** is to leave a country in order to live in another. Unfortunately, many nations' hopes for the future depend on the young.

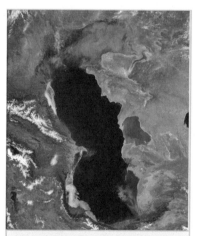

This photo of the Caspian Sea was taken from space.

My World Geography Vocabulary

Go to page 97 to list other words you have learned about Central Asia.

landlocked	precipitation	earthquake	nomad	Silk Road
arid	erosion	tribe	tradition	emigrate

A. *Fill in the blanks with the correct vocabulary word.*

1. a shaking of part of Earth's surface as a result of underground forces

   — — — — — — — — — —

2. a person who travels from place to place, in search of food or grazing for animals

   — — — — —

3. surrounded by land

   — — — — — — — — — —

4. to leave a country in order to live in another

   — — — — — — — —

5. the wearing away of land

   — — — — — — —

6. water that falls to Earth as rain or snow

   — — — — — — — — — — — — —

7. a belief or custom handed down from one generation to the next

   — — — — — — — — —

8. a trade route that went from China, through Central Asia, to the Mediterranean Sea

   — — — —   — — — —

9. dry

   — — — —

10. a group of people who share a way of life

    — — — — —

| landlocked | precipitation | earthquake | nomad | Silk Road |
| arid | erosion | tribe | tradition | emigrate |

B. *Choose and write the two words that best complete each sentence.*

| arid | tradition | landlocked | nomad |

1. A wandering desert _____ would never see an ocean

   because Central Asia is _____ .

| precipitation | emigrate | erosion | arid |

2. If the land is _____ , it will not get much

   _____ in the form of rain or snow.

| landlocked | erosion | earthquake | tribe |

3. The land's surface might be worn down by _____ or

   moved by an _____ .

| nomad | Silk Road | tribe | precipitation |

4. Traders along the _____ might have met a

   _____ and exchanged goods with its members.

| tradition | emigrate | earthquake | Silk Road |

5. After people _____ from their country, they might no

   longer care about a _____ they once held dear.

ROOT

The word **nomad** comes from the Greek word **nomas**, which referred to a wandering group of people.

landlocked	precipitation	earthquake	nomad	Silk Road
arid	erosion	tribe	tradition	emigrate

C. *Choose the correct vocabulary word to complete each sentence.*

1. A trade route called the _____ once cut across Central Asia.

2. To find grass for his animals, a _____ must keep moving from one place to the next.

3. Heavy rain can wash away the soil and cause _____ .

4. Some people want to _____ from Central Asia because life there is so hard.

5. It might be a _____ for a tribe to welcome strangers with a special meal.

6. Much damage and loss of life can be caused by an _____ .

7. Crops will not grow unless there is warm weather, good soil, and enough

   _____ .

8. In a _____ country, people cannot meet outsiders in a port city.

9. Many things will not grow in an _____ climate because of the lack of rain.

10. All the members of the _____ spoke the same language.

| landlocked | precipitation | earthquake | nomad | Silk Road |
| arid | erosion | tribe | tradition | emigrate |

D. *Use each word in a sentence that shows you understand the meaning of each word.*

1. earthquake _____

   _____

2. erosion _____

   _____

3. emigrate _____

   _____

4. arid _____

   _____

5. nomad _____

   _____

6. landlocked _____

   _____

7. precipitation _____

   _____

8. tribe _____

   _____

9. Silk Road _____

   _____

10. tradition _____

    _____

Write! _____

Write your response to the prompt on a separate sheet of paper.
Use as many vocabulary words as you can in your writing.

Describe how the land and people of Central Asia are linked.

subcontinent   Hinduism   Buddhism   Green Revolution
monsoon   reincarnation   pagoda   information technology
dialect   caste

South Asia has a rich past and an exciting future. Read this selection to learn about the land and people of South Asia.

South Asia

A Subcontinent

Mountains and deserts cut off South Asia from the rest of Asia. That makes South Asia a subcontinent. A **subcontinent** is a large area cut off from the rest of a continent by land features.

Climate varies across South Asia. Much of India is affected by monsoons. A **monsoon** is a seasonal wind that changes direction twice a year. When the winds blow in from the ocean, they bring rain. When they blow from the land to the ocean, they bring cool, dry weather.

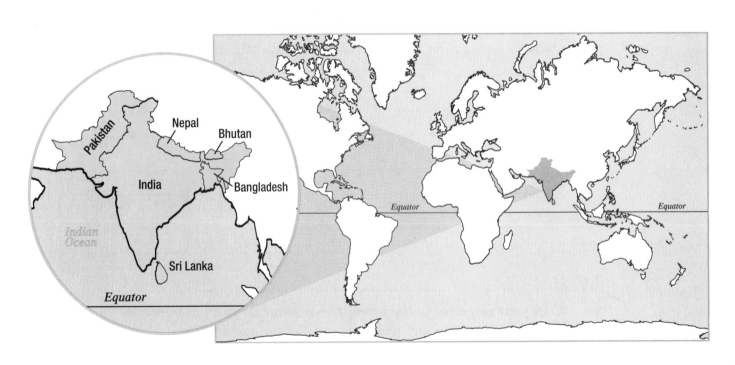

The People

About 16 major languages are spoken in South Asia. But there are hundreds of dialects. A **dialect** is a different form of the same language. Urdu, for example, is the national language of Pakistan. It has at least four different dialects.

The main religion in India is **Hinduism**. A belief in many gods and in reincarnation are central to Hinduism. **Reincarnation** is the idea that each soul must be reborn many times. A person's good deeds in one life may give him or her a better life in the next.

Lakshmi is the Hindu goddess of wealth and happiness.

Hinduism also teaches respect for one's caste. A **caste** is a social group one is born into and cannot change. A person's caste determines what jobs and friends a person can have. In Hinduism, people are born into one of four castes. There is also a fifth group— "Untouchables." Hindus once considered them less than human.

Buddhism is popular in the South Asian countries of Nepal, Sri Lanka, and Bhutan. **Buddhism** is a religion that began in India. Buddhism teaches that people are too attached to the things of this world. Buddhists believe that good deeds will end suffering.

Buddhists practice their teachings in buildings called temples. Some temples are pagodas. A **pagoda** is a tower built with many stories, or levels.

This pagoda is found at a Buddhist temple in Nepal.

Most people in Pakistan and Bangladesh are followers of Islam.

Changing Times

Most people in South Asia live in villages and farm. Many cannot read or write. But more children are getting an education. The Green Revolution has made many lives better. The **Green Revolution** is a movement aimed at improving farming methods and crop yields.

Industry is growing in South Asia. India's fastest-growing industry is **information technology**. It is the use of computer hardware, software, and the Internet to help people to process information.

India is a leader in information technology.

My World Geography Vocabulary

Go to page 97 to list other words you have learned about South Asia.

subcontinent	Hinduism	Buddhism	Green Revolution
monsoon	reincarnation	pagoda	information technology
dialect	caste		

A. *Match each word with its meaning. Write the letter of the correct meaning on the line in front of each word.*

1. _____ Buddhism

2. _____ caste

3. _____ pagoda

4. _____ Green Revolution

5. _____ subcontinent

6. _____ Hinduism

7. _____ information technology

8. _____ dialect

9. _____ reincarnation

10. _____ monsoon

a. an Indian religion based on the belief in many gods and reincarnation

b. a religion that began in India that teaches that people are too attached to the things of this world

c. the use of computer hardware, software, and the Internet to help people to process information

d. a seasonal wind that changes direction twice a year

e. a movement aimed to improve farming methods and crop yields

f. a social group one is born into and cannot change

g. a different form of the same language

h. a tower with many stories or levels often used as a temple

i. a large part of a continent that is separated from the rest of the continent by land features

j. the idea that each soul must be reborn many times

66

subcontinent	Hinduism	Buddhism	Green Revolution
monsoon	reincarnation	pagoda	information technology
dialect	caste		

B. *Circle the word that makes sense in each sentence. Then write the word.*

1. India's fastest growing industry is (dialect, information technology).

   _____

2. A belief of (Buddhism, Hinduism) is that owning things causes unhappiness.

   _____

3. A soul is reborn during (Green Revolution, reincarnation).

   _____

4. Many Buddhist temples take the form of a (pagoda, dialect).

   _____

5. Rain often follows a (monsoon, subcontinent). _____

6. Crop yields increased after the (information technology, Green Revolution).

   _____

7. My mother and father speak a different (caste, dialect) of the same language.

   _____

8. Landforms create the (monsoon, subcontinent) on which India is located.

   _____

9. Ideas about social castes are part of (Hinduism, pagoda).

   _____

10. A person's social (caste, reincarnation) can determine his or her work.

    _____

WORD ROOT

The word **dialect** has its roots in the Greek word **dialektos**, which means "conversation."

subcontinent	Hinduism	Buddhism	Green Revolution
monsoon	reincarnation	pagoda	information technology
dialect	caste		

C. *Write the vocabulary word that best completes each pair of sentences.*

1. The most popular religion in India is _____ .

   A belief in castes is part of _____ .

2. A Buddhist temple may take the form of a _____ .

   A tower in Asia with many levels might be a _____ .

3. Farmers were helped by the _____ .

   People had more food after the _____ .

4. Followers of _____ believe good deeds end suffering.

   Many people in Nepal are believers in _____ .

5. Landforms that act as barriers create a _____ .

   India is a country on the South Asia _____ .

6. India's fastest growing industry is _____ .

   Computer hardware, software, and the Internet are part of

   _____ .

7. Hindus believe that souls are reborn during _____ .

   Several different religions believe in _____ .

8. A _____ is a variety of a language.

   A person might speak more than one _____ of a language.

9. A wind that changes direction is a _____ .

   A change of season can be brought about by a _____ .

10. In Hinduism, a person is born into a _____ that cannot
    change.

    A social group to which a Hindu belongs for life is a _____ .

South Asia

subcontinent	Hinduism	Buddhism	Green Revolution
monsoon	reincarnation	pagoda	information technology
dialect	caste		

D. *Use each word in a sentence that shows you understand the meaning of each word.*

1. Green Revolution _____

   _____

2. Buddhism _____

   _____

3. caste _____

   _____

4. dialect _____

   _____

5. Hinduism _____

   _____

6. information technology _____

   _____

7. subcontinent _____

   _____

8. monsoon _____

   _____

9. pagoda _____

   _____

10. reincarnation _____

    _____

Write! _____

Write your response to the prompt on a separate sheet of paper.
Use as many vocabulary words as you can in your writing.

How is South Asia different from other places you have read about?

archipelago   Ring of Fire   typhoon   paddy   port
inhabited   tsunami   cultivation   terrace farming   strait

You probably wear or own more than one thing made in Southeast Asia. Read this selection to learn about the land and people in this area.

Southeast Asia

Extreme Nature

Southeast Asia includes part of mainland Asia and the Malay Archipelago. An **archipelago** is a group of many islands. The country of Indonesia includes about 17,000 islands. Only 6,000 are **inhabited**, or have people living on them. The island area is part of the Ring of Fire. The **Ring of Fire** is an area of volcanic activity along the Pacific Ocean. At least one volcano erupts here every year.

This is also an area of earthquakes. Sometimes they cause a **tsunami**. That is a huge sea wave caused by an underwater earthquake. A tsunami can be 200 feet high and travel as fast as a jet! When a tsunami hits the shore, it causes much damage.

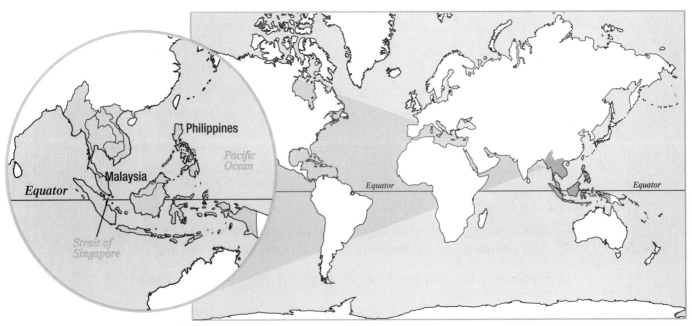

The climate is hot and moist. The rain that comes with seasonal winds floods the area. Typhoons destroy everything in their path. A **typhoon** is a violent storm that occurs in the Pacific Ocean. Wind speeds can reach more than 200 miles per hour!

Cultivating the Land

Most people farm small plots of land. The warm climate and seasonal rains are just right for the cultivation of certain crops. **Cultivation** is the act of preparing land and growing crops. For example, when fields are flooded, people plant rice. In Southeast Asia, rice is grown in paddies. A **paddy** is a flooded field.

In hilly areas, people practice **terrace farming**. That is the growing of crops on step-like levels cut into the soil. When it rains, the terrace prevents the soil from washing away. Many people also have small boats and fish. Some even live on their boats.

Terrace farming allows farmers to catch and use water that flows down hills.

Cities

Foreign countries have factories in Southeast Asia because of the low cost of labor. Cities have grown up around factories. Cities in Southeast Asia are different from those in other parts of the world. Many people get around on bicycles, not cars. The crime rate is low. The streets are clean. Living spaces are very small.

Singapore is the name of both a tiny country and a modern port city. A **port** is a place where ships can dock. Raw materials come into the port. Finished goods from factories leave the port. Ship traffic through the Singapore Strait is brisk. A **strait** is a narrow strip of water between large areas of land.

Many Americans buy goods made in Southeast Asia. The shoes you're wearing might well have been made there!

Boats and ships travel down the Singapore Strait.

My World Geography Vocabulary

Go to page 97 to list other words you have learned about Southeast Asia.

archipelago   **Ring of Fire**   typhoon   **paddy**   port

inhabited   tsunami   cultivation   terrace farming   strait

A. *Fill in the blanks with the correct vocabulary word.*

1. a huge sea wave caused by an underwater earthquake

    — — — — — — —

2. the growing of crops on step-like levels cut into the soil

    — — — — — — —   — — — — — — —

3. a narrow strip of water between large areas of land

    — — — — — —

4. having people living in a place

    — — — — — — — — —

5. a violent storm that occurs in the Pacific Ocean

    — — — — — — —

6. a flooded field where rice is grown

    — — — — —

7. a group of islands

    — — — — — — — — — — —

8. a place where ships can dock

    — — — —

9. the act of preparing land and growing crops

    — — — — — — — — — — —

10. an area of volcanic activity along the Pacific Ocean

    — — — —   — —   — — — —

Southeast Asia

archipelago	Ring of Fire	typhoon	paddy	port
inhabited	tsunami	cultivation	terrace farming	strait

B. *Circle the word that makes sense in each sentence. Then write the word.*

1. Strong winds blow in a (port, typhoon). _____

2. Ships dock in a (Ring of Fire, port). _____

3. A very high wave may be a (tsunami, strait). _____

4. Ships go through a (paddy, strait). _____

5. There are volcanoes in the (Ring of Fire, tsunami). _____

6. Many islands make up an (inhabited, archipelago).

   _____

7. Growing crops on levels of earth is (terrace farming, typhoon).

   _____

8. Rice grows in a (paddy, archipelago). _____

9. The (port, cultivation) of rice is suited to warm, wet areas.

   _____

10. A place with people and their homes is (inhabited, cultivation).

    _____

ROOT

The word **inhabited** comes from the Latin word **habitare**, which means "to live in."

archipelago   Ring of Fire   typhoon   paddy   port

inhabited   tsunami   cultivation   terrace farming   strait

C. *Choose the correct vocabulary word to complete each sentence.*

1. Singapore has a _____ where ships can dock.

2. A narrow body of water between two landmasses is a

   _____ .

3. A flooded field where rice grows is a _____ .

4. Many islands form an _____ .

5. An area along the Pacific with many volcanoes is called the

   _____ .

6. Growing crops on steps cut into a hillside is _____ .

7. Rain and warm weather are needed for the _____ of rice.

8. An island with people living on it is _____ .

9. An earthquake under the ocean might cause a _____ .

10. A violent storm in the Pacific Ocean is called a _____ .

| archipelago | Ring of Fire | typhoon | paddy | port |
| inhabited | tsunami | cultivation | terrace farming | strait |

D. *Use each word in a sentence that shows you understand the meaning of each word.*

1. Ring of Fire _____

_____

2. tsunami _____

_____

3. strait _____

_____

4. archipelago _____

_____

5. port _____

_____

6. inhabited _____

_____

7. terrace farming _____

_____

8. paddy _____

_____

9. cultivation _____

_____

10. typhoon _____

_____

Write! _____

Write your response to the prompt on a separate sheet of paper.
Use as many vocabulary words as you can in your writing.

What is unusual about Southeast Asia?

Southeast Asia

isolation   calligraphy   global economy   trade surplus
homogeneous society   kabuki   interdependence   trade deficit
haiku   martial arts

The countries in East Asia are different from other Asian countries.
Read this passage to find out about those differences.

East Asia

Isolation

East Asia includes a mainland and islands. Some countries, such as Japan, developed in isolation. **Isolation** means cut off from other areas and people. The Japanese had little contact with outsiders. They developed a **homogeneous society**. That is a society made up of mostly the same kind of people. They look similar and have the same culture.

Japanese Culture

Japanese people value beauty and simplicity in their arts. For example, a **haiku** is a traditional Japanese poem. It is written in three lines. The lines have five, seven, and five syllables. These poems usually focus on nature or the poet's feelings.

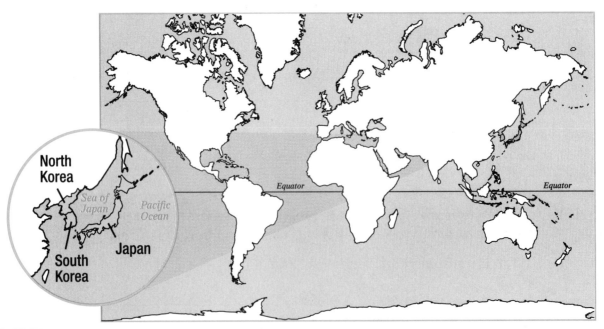

East Asia

Many Japanese arts have roots in China. **Calligraphy**, the art of beautiful writing, began in China. Japanese artists soon developed their own style. Today, Japanese children study calligraphy in school.

This elementary school student practices calligraphy.

Kabuki is a form of Japanese drama. It combines singing, dancing, bold makeup, and elaborate costumes.

Many Americans have watched movies showing Japanese **martial arts**. They are traditional forms of fighting and exercise that use the hands and feet.

A Global Economy

Japan and South Korea are part of a **global economy**. They trade with many countries. Their economies are based on interdependence. **Interdependence** means that countries rely on and affect each other. If one country has money problems, it affects other countries too.

Until recently, North Korea traded with few other countries. Most of its people are farmers. They were not able to grow enough food to feed everyone. Many North Koreans went hungry.

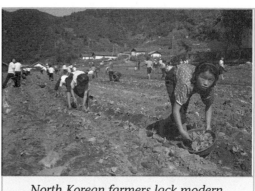

North Korean farmers lack modern farm machinery.

Countries need to trade goods to keep their economies strong. A **trade surplus** happens when there are more exports than imports. A **trade deficit** happens when there are more imports than exports. Countries must be able to buy goods they need—and have money to pay for them.

South Korea and Japan have a trade surplus with the United States. They export more goods to the United States than they import.

My World Geography Vocabulary

Go to page 98 to list other words you have learned about East Asia.

isolation	calligraphy	global economy	trade surplus
homogeneous society	kabuki	interdependence	trade deficit
haiku	martial arts		

A. *Match each word with its meaning. Write the letter of the correct meaning on the line in front of each word.*

1. _____ interdependence

2. _____ kabuki

3. _____ haiku

4. _____ global economy

5. _____ trade deficit

6. _____ isolation

7. _____ calligraphy

8. _____ trade surplus

9. _____ martial arts

10. _____ homogeneous society

a. a society made up of mostly the same kind of people

b. forms of fighting that mainly use the hands and feet

c. a result of more exports than imports

d. cut off from other areas and people

e. an economy that is international

f. the art of writing beautifully

g. a form of Japanese drama that combines singing, dancing, bold makeup, and elaborate costumes

h. a traditional Japanese poem written in three lines

i. a result of more imports than exports

j. a state of relying on and affecting many others

isolation	calligraphy	global economy	trade surplus
homogeneous society	kabuki	interdependence	trade deficit
haiku	martial arts		

B. *Choose and write the two words that best complete each sentence.*

| interdependence | isolation | trade deficit | trade surplus |

1. Having more imports than exports is a _____ ; the opposite is a _____ .

| haiku | trade deficit | isolation | homogeneous society |

2. Japan has a _____ as a result of _____ from the rest of the world.

| interdependence | trade surplus | global economy | isolation |

3. Countries in a _____ have an _____ on other countries in that same economy.

| martial arts | kabuki | calligraphy | homogeneous society |

4. Forms of Japanese fighting are called _____ ; a form of Japanese theater is _____ .

| martial arts | kabuki | calligraphy | haiku |

5. A short Japanese poem called a _____ might be written using _____ .

WORD ROOT

The word **calligraphy** comes from the Greek words **kallos**, which means "beauty" and **graphein**, which means "write."

isolation	calligraphy	global economy	trade surplus
homogeneous society	kabuki	interdependence	trade deficit
haiku	martial arts		

C. *Choose the correct vocabulary word to complete each sentence.*

1. When more than two countries' economies affect each other, that creates an

    _____ .

2. A poem that has three lines with five, seven, and five syllables is a

    _____ .

3. A country in _____ has no outside contact.

4. Fancy stage sets are part of _____ .

5. If Japan sold more goods to other countries than it bought, it would have a

    _____ .

6. American movies made _____ fighting popular.

7. If South Korea bought more goods from other countries than it sold, it would

    have a _____ .

8. When people have the same looks and beliefs, they form a

    _____ .

9. A worldwide economy is a _____ .

10. The Japanese create beautiful writing called _____

    with a brush and black ink.

isolation	calligraphy	global economy	trade surplus
homogeneous society	kabuki	interdependence	trade deficit
haiku	martial arts		

D. *Use each word in a sentence that shows you understand the meaning of each word.*

1. martial arts _____

   _____

2. kabuki _____

   _____

3. trade surplus _____

   _____

4. calligraphy _____

   _____

5. haiku _____

   _____

6. isolation _____

   _____

7. trade deficit _____

   _____

8. interdependence _____

   _____

9. homogeneous society _____

   _____

10. global economy _____

   _____

Write! _____

Write your response to the prompt on a separate sheet of paper.
Use as many vocabulary words as you can in your writing.

Would you like to visit East Asia? Why or why not?

distribution   gorge   hydroelectricity   Taoism   repression
fossil fuels   reservoir   Confucianism   acid rain   human rights

China has one of the oldest cultures in the world. Yet it has modern problems. Read this selection to learn about China.

China

Changing the Land

China is the largest country in East Asia. It has mountain ranges, deserts, plateaus, and rivers. It has natural resources, too. However, their **distribution**, or spread, throughout China is not equal.

The 4,000-mile Yangtze River is one natural resource. But it floods often. In the last 100 years, its floods have killed one million people. Another natural resource is coal. China burns about 50 million tons of coal each year. However, supplies of this fossil fuel are limited. **Fossil fuels** include coal, oil, and natural gas. They formed millions of years ago from the remains of living things.

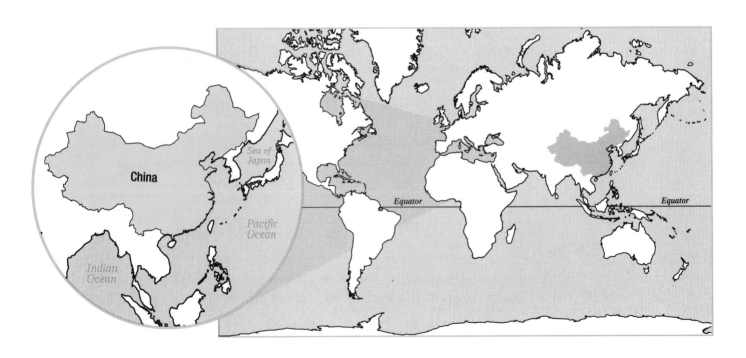

Changing the Land

The government wants to control flooding. It also wants to cut the use of coal. So it built the largest dam in the world. The dam is 1.5 miles wide and 600 feet high. It is called the Three Gorges Dam, after the natural gorges in the area. A **gorge** is a canyon with steep walls.

The dam holds back water from the Yangtze River in a reservoir. A **reservoir** is a lake that people have made to store water. The reservoir is 400 miles long. The dam provides **hydroelectricity**. That is energy created by water allowed to fall over a dam. When the dam is working fully, it will supply one-ninth of China's energy.

More than one million people had to move to make way for the Three Gorges Dam and its reservoir.

People's Beliefs

China is home to more than one billion people. About 94 percent of them belong to the same ethnic group. Many follow **Confucianism**. This belief system stresses the value of family and the duties that people owe each other. Respect for the elderly and education are highly valued.

Many people also follow **Taoism**. This belief system stresses finding inner peace and accepting change.

China's Problems

China is working to become modern. In doing so, it has created problems. Burning coal pollutes the air. Then acid rain falls. **Acid rain** is rain that carries pollution in the air to the ground. Acid rain harms plants and crops.

Followers of Confucianism built this temple in China.

Another problem is government repression. **Repression** is the putting down of citizens' human rights. **Human rights** are rights that every person should have. They include freedom of speech and religion. For years, people who spoke or wrote anything that disagreed with government policy were treated badly. They were put in prison or killed.

My World Geography Vocabulary

Go to page 98 to list other words you have learned about China.

distribution   gorge   hydroelectricity   Taoism   repression

fossil fuels   reservoir   Confucianism   acid rain   human rights

A.   *Fill in the blanks with the correct vocabulary word.*

1.   the putting down of citizen's human rights

— — — — — — — — — —

2.   a belief system that stresses the value of family and the duties that
     people owe each other

— — — — — — — — — — — —

3.   rain that carries air pollution to the ground

— — — —   — — — —

4.   a lake that people have made to store water

— — — — — — — — —

5.   a belief system that stresses finding inner peace and accepting change

— — — — — —

6.   a canyon with steep walls

— — — — —

7.   energy created by water falling over a dam

— — — — — — — — — — — — — — — —

8.   coal, oil, or natural gas that formed millions of years ago

— — — — — —   — — — — —

9.   rights that every person should have

— — — — —   — — — — — —

10. the spread of something throughout an area

— — — — — — — — — — — — —

84

distribution   gorge   hydroelectricity   Taoism   repression

fossil fuels   reservoir   Confucianism   acid rain   human rights

B. *Circle the word that makes sense in each sentence. Then write the word.*

1. A lake behind a dam is a (acid rain, reservoir). _____

2. A belief system that tells how to live a responsible life is (Taoism, Confucianism).
    _____

3. A belief system that stresses accepting change is (Taoism, Confucianism).
    _____

4. Gas and oil are (hydroelectricity, fossil fuels). _____

5. The way in which things are spread out is their (repression, distribution).
    _____

6. Rights that everyone should have are (human rights, distribution).
    _____

7. A steep-sided canyon is a (reservoir, gorge). _____

8. Not letting someone speak up is (repression, human rights).
    _____

9. Some pollution is brought to Earth by (acid rain, gorge).
    _____

10. Dams make (fossil fuels, hydroelectricity). _____

ROOT

The word **fossil** comes from the Latin word **fossilis**, which means "something that is dug up."

distribution   gorge   hydroelectricity   Taoism   repression

fossil fuels   reservoir   Confucianism   acid rain   human rights

C. *Write the vocabulary word that best completes each pair of sentences.*

1. Pollution comes to Earth in _____ .

   Burning coal leads to _____ .

2. Dams make _____ .

   One form of power from water is _____ .

3. A canyon with steep walls is a _____ .

   It would be hard to climb out of a _____ .

4. People who believe in _____ accept change.

   One belief system in China is called _____ .

5. Not giving people their rights is _____ .

   Not letting people state their opinions is _____ .

6. Coal and oil are _____ .

   Burning _____ makes pollution.

7. The _____ of China's resources is not equal.

   The spread of things is their _____ .

8. The water held back by a dam is a _____ .

   A lake made by people can be used as a _____ .

9. Freedom of speech and religion are two _____ .

   China does not always give its citizens _____ .

10. A belief system that values family relations is _____ .

    Respect for the elderly is part of _____ .

China

| distribution | gorge | hydroelectricity | Taoism | repression |
| fossil fuels | reservoir | Confucianism | acid rain | human rights |

D. *Use each word in a sentence that shows you understand the meaning of the word.*

1. Confucianism _____

_____

2. hydroelectricity _____

_____

3. human rights _____

_____

4. distribution _____

_____

5. fossil fuels _____

_____

6. repression _____

_____

7. acid rain _____

_____

8. reservoir _____

_____

9. Taoism _____

_____

10. gorge _____

_____

 ***Write!*** _____

Write your response to the prompt on a separate sheet of paper.
Use as many vocabulary words as you can in your writing.

What might be the solutions to some of China's problems?

There are thousands of islands in the Pacific Ocean. One is a continent. Others are tiny. Read this selection to learn more about them.

Oceania, Australia, and Antarctica

Special Lands and Creatures

Oceania includes the islands and archipelagos of the Pacific Ocean. Oceania has many small colonies of coral. Coral are small sea creatures. Sometimes, the colonies form an atoll. An **atoll** is a ring-shaped coral island. Atolls are not much above sea level.

In time, many atolls might form a coral reef. A **coral reef** is an ocean barrier. It is made up of the hard skeletons of billions of coral. Such a reef is parallel to the shore. The Great Barrier Reef in Australia is 1,250 miles long! A **lagoon** is a shallow area of ocean water. It is often found between a coral reef and the shore. A lagoon may also be found in the middle of an atoll.

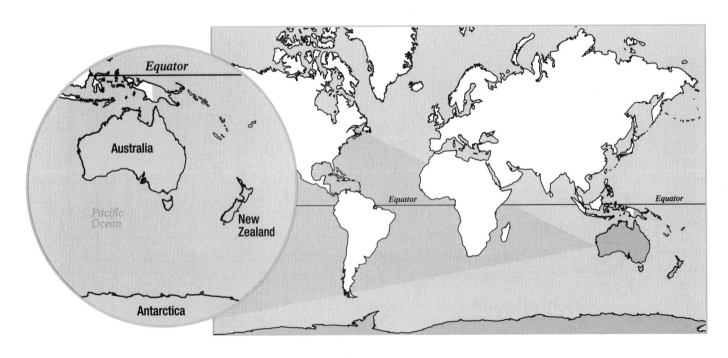

A coral reef is home to many species. A **species** is a separate kind of plant or animal. The Great Barrier Reef has 200 species of birds. It has more than 1,500 species of fish. Australia also has unusual land species. Kangaroos and koala bears are found only in Australia.

Penguins live in Antarctica. People do not. It is **frigid**, or extremely cold. Winds can blow at more than 100 miles per hour. Almost all of Antarctica is covered by an ice cap. An **ice cap** is a thick layer of ice and snow.

Many different species of shark live in the Great Barrier Reef.

Australia's First People

Aborigines, Australia's first people, arrived more than 30,000 years ago. In the late 1700s, Europeans came to Australia. Today, 85 percent of Australians live in cities. Others live in the outback. The **outback** is the dry plains in the center of Australia. People there graze sheep on the sparse grass.

These Aborigines presented a concert of native music in Australia.

Challenges of Global Warming

Global warming is the rise in the temperature of Earth's lands and oceans. Warmer ocean water is killing coral reefs. It is also melting Antarctica's ice. Melting ice causes oceans to rise. Warmer temperatures are also killing indigenous animals. **Indigenous** means "natural or native to a place." It refers to the people, plants, or animals that arose there.

Climate change affects people too. The world is having extreme weather. Scientists around the world agree. We must work together to stop global warming.

My World Geography Vocabulary

Go to page 98 to list other words you have learned about Oceania, Australia, and Antarctica.

atoll   lagoon   frigid   Aborigines   global warming

coral reef   species   ice cap   outback   indigenous

A. *Match each word with its meaning. Write the letter of the correct meaning on the line in front of each word.*

1. ____ species

2. ____ ice cap

3. ____ outback

4. ____ atoll

5. ____ global warming

6. ____ frigid

7. ____ coral reef

8. ____ indigenous

9. ____ Aborigines

10. ____ lagoon

a. the dry plains in the center of Australia

b. extremely cold

c. the rise in the temperature of Earth's lands and oceans

d. an ocean barrier made up of the hard skeletons of billions of coral

e. a thick layer of ice and snow

f. Australia's first people

g. natural or native to a place

h. a ring-shaped coral island that does not rise much above sea level

i. the shallow ocean water between a coral reef and the shore

j. a separate kind of living thing

Oceania, Australia, and Antarctica

| atoll | lagoon | frigid | Aborigines | global warming |
| coral reef | species | ice cap | outback | indigenous |

B. *Choose and write the two words that best complete each sentence.*

| coral reef | frigid | atoll | ice cap |

1. Antarctica is a _____ continent mostly covered by an

    _____ .

| coral reef | indigenous | species | atoll |

2. Fish of many different _____ live in a

    _____ .

| Aborigines | lagoon | outback | global warming |

3. The first people to live in Australia's _____ were

    _____ .

| global warming | frigid | Aborigines | indigenous |

4. Animals that are _____ to Australia and Antarctica are

    being killed by _____ .

| lagoon | ice cap | atoll | outback |

5. A large _____ might surround a shallow

    _____ .

WORD ROOT

The word **species** has its roots in the Latin word **species**, which means "kind" or "sort."

atoll	lagoon	frigid	Aborigines	global warming
coral reef	species	ice cap	outback	indigenous

C. *Write the vocabulary word that best completes each pair of sentences.*

1. The first Australians were ＿＿＿＿＿＿＿＿＿＿ .

   ＿＿＿＿＿＿＿＿＿＿ know how to survive in the outback.

2. Antarctica is mostly covered by an ＿＿＿＿＿＿＿＿＿＿ .

   An ＿＿＿＿＿＿＿＿＿＿ is made of ice and snow.

3. Animals are being killed by ＿＿＿＿＿＿＿＿＿＿ .

   Many countries want to stop ＿＿＿＿＿＿＿＿＿＿ .

4. Australia's plains are called the ＿＿＿＿＿＿＿＿＿＿ .

   Sheep eat the grass on Australia's ＿＿＿＿＿＿＿＿＿＿ .

5. Global warming is killing many ＿＿＿＿＿＿＿＿＿＿ of plants.

   A coral reef is home to many ＿＿＿＿＿＿＿＿＿＿ of fish.

6. The Great Barrier Reef is a ＿＿＿＿＿＿＿＿＿＿ .

   Billions of coral skeletons make up a ＿＿＿＿＿＿＿＿＿＿ .

7. A temperature of −94°F would feel ＿＿＿＿＿＿＿＿＿＿ .

   Weather in Antarctica is ＿＿＿＿＿＿＿＿＿＿ .

8. A small coral island is an ＿＿＿＿＿＿＿＿＿＿ .

   An ＿＿＿＿＿＿＿＿＿＿ is just above sea level.

9. The shore and the reef are separated by a ＿＿＿＿＿＿＿＿＿＿ .

   An atoll might have a ＿＿＿＿＿＿＿＿＿＿ in its center.

10. A kangaroo is ＿＿＿＿＿＿＿＿＿＿ to Australia.

    Some of Australia's ＿＿＿＿＿＿＿＿＿＿ animal species are seen nowhere else.

atoll	lagoon	frigid	Aborigines	global warming
coral reef	species	ice cap	outback	indigenous

D. *Use each pair of words in a sentence.*

1. global warming, ice cap

   _____

   _____

   _____

2. frigid, coral reef

   _____

   _____

   _____

3. Aborigines, outback

   _____

   _____

   _____

4. indigenous, species

   _____

   _____

   _____

5. lagoon, atoll

   _____

   _____

   _____

Write!

**Write your response to the prompt on a separate sheet of paper.
Use as many vocabulary words as you can in your writing.**

Imagine that you could spend a week exploring any place in this region.
Where would you go? Why?

My Social Studies Vocabulary

Lesson 1: Geography—Looking at the World

_____   _____   _____

_____   _____   _____

_____   _____   _____

_____   _____   _____

_____   _____   _____

Lesson 2: The Tools of Geography

_____   _____   _____

_____   _____   _____

_____   _____   _____

_____   _____   _____

_____   _____   _____

Lesson 3: World Cultures

_____   _____   _____

_____   _____   _____

_____   _____   _____

_____   _____   _____

My Social Studies Vocabulary

Lesson 4: The United States and Canada

_____   _____   _____

_____   _____   _____

_____   _____   _____

_____   _____   _____

_____   _____   _____

Lesson 5: Latin America

_____   _____   _____

_____   _____   _____

_____   _____   _____

_____   _____   _____

_____   _____   _____

Lesson 6: Europe

_____   _____   _____

_____   _____   _____

_____   _____   _____

_____   _____   _____

_____   _____   _____

Lesson 7: Russia

_____ _____ _____

_____ _____ _____

_____ _____ _____

_____ _____ _____

_____ _____ _____

Lesson 8: North Africa and Southwest Asia

_____ _____ _____

_____ _____ _____

_____ _____ _____

_____ _____ _____

_____ _____ _____

Lesson 9: Africa South of the Sahara

_____ _____ _____

_____ _____ _____

_____ _____ _____

_____ _____ _____

My Social Studies Vocabulary

Lesson 10: Central Asia

_____   _____   _____

_____   _____   _____

_____   _____   _____

_____   _____   _____

_____   _____   _____

Lesson 11: South Asia

_____   _____   _____

_____   _____   _____

_____   _____   _____

_____   _____   _____

_____   _____   _____

Lesson 12: Southeast Asia

_____   _____   _____

_____   _____   _____

_____   _____   _____

_____   _____   _____

_____   _____   _____

Lesson 13: East Asia

_____   _____   _____

_____   _____   _____

_____   _____   _____

_____   _____   _____

_____   _____   _____

Lesson 14: China

_____   _____   _____

_____   _____   _____

_____   _____   _____

_____   _____   _____

_____   _____   _____

Lesson 15: Oceania, Australia, and Antarctica

_____   _____   _____

_____   _____   _____

_____   _____   _____

_____   _____   _____

_____   _____   _____

Root Words

A word that is the beginning, or source, of a new word is called a "root word." Many English words have roots in other languages. Latin and Greek are two languages that have given English many new words. The study of geography is rich in words that come to English from these languages. The word *geography* itself comes from the Greek word *geographia*, which means "description of the earth."

This chart shows some Greek and Latin roots, their meanings, and examples of English words that use the roots. Use the space provided to write other words with the same roots and to add new roots, meanings, and examples.

Latin or Greek Root	Meaning	Examples
vegetare	grow	vegetation, _____, _____, _____
theos	god	theocracy, _____, _____, _____
populus	people	population, _____, _____, _____
_____	_____	_____, _____
_____	_____	_____, _____
_____	_____	_____, _____
_____	_____	_____, _____
_____	_____	_____, _____

Prefixes and Suffixes

Prefixes

A prefix is a group of letters added to the beginning of a word to change the meaning. For example, *un-* is a prefix that means "not." Adding *un-* to *clear* makes the word *unclear*, which means "not clear." Add your own prefixes, meanings, and examples in the space below.

Prefix	Meaning	Examples
over-	too much	overpopulation, _____ , _____
sub-	under	subsistence, _____ , _____
inter-	between	interdependence, _____ , _____
_____	_____	_____ , _____ , _____
_____	_____	_____ , _____ , _____

Suffixes

A suffix is a group of letters added to the end of a word to change the meaning. For example, *-er* is a suffix that means "one who." Adding *-er* to *teach* makes the word *teacher*, which means "one who teaches." Add your own suffixes, meanings, and examples in the spaces below.

Suffix	Meaning	Examples
-ment	action, state	government, _____ , _____
-logy	science or state of	technology, _____ , _____
-ism	belief or theory	Taoism, _____ , _____
_____	_____	_____ , _____ , _____
_____	_____	_____ , _____ , _____

Glossary

Aa

Aborigines (ab-uh-RIHJ-uh-nees)
the first people of Australia
(Lesson 15, page 89)

absolute location
(AB-suh-loot loh-KAY-shuhn)
a place's exact location on a grid of latitude
and longitude
(Lesson 2, page 11)

acid rain (AS-ihd rayn)
rain that carries pollution in the air to the
ground
(Lesson 14, page 83)

agriculture
(AG-ruh-kuhl-chuhr)
the growing of crops
(Lesson 1, page 5)

arable (AR-uh-buhl)
suitable for use as farmland
(Lesson 8, page 47)

archipelago
(ahr-kuh-PEHL-uh-goh)
a group of many islands
(Lesson 12, page 70)

arid (AR-ihd)
dry
(Lesson 10, page 58)

atoll

atoll (AT-ol)
a ring-shaped
coral island that
does not rise much
above sea level
(Lesson 15, page 88)

Bb

border (BAWR-duhr)
an imaginary line that separates countries
(Lesson 6, page 35)

Buddhism (BUD-ihz-uhm)
the religion that began in India that teaches
that people are too attached to the things
of this world
(Lesson 11, page 65)

Cc

calligraphy
(kuh-LIHG-ruh-fee)
the art of beautiful
writing
(Lesson 13, page 77)

capitalism
(KAP-uh-tuh-lihz-uhm)
an economic system in which private owners
control and use resources for profit
(Lesson 4, page 23)

cash crop (kash krop)
a crop that is raised to sell
(Lesson 5, page 29)

caste (kast)

a social group one is born into and cannot change

(Lesson 11, page 65)

channel (CHAN-uhl)

a narrow sea between two large areas of land

(Lesson 6, page 34)

civilization (sihv-uh-luh-ZAY-shuhn)

a large, organized group of people

(Lesson 1, page 5)

clan (klan)

a group of people who are related

(Lesson 9, page 53)

climate (KLY-miht)

the weather in an area over a period of time

(Lesson 1, page 4)

collective farm (kuh-LEHK-tihv fahrm)

a farm that the Soviet government owned and managed

(Lesson 7, page 41)

colonization (kol-uh-nuh-ZAY-shuhn)

the making of settlements in another land

(Lesson 5, page 29)

command economy

(kuh-MAND ih-KON-uh-mee)

an economy in which the government decides what to produce, not the people or business owners

(Lesson 7, page 41)

common currency

(KOM-uhn KUR-uhn-see)

a system of money that is shared by different countries

(Lesson 6, page 35)

communism (KOM-yuh-nihz-uhm)

an economic system in which the government owns all property and businesses

(Lesson 7, page 41)

Confucianism

(kuhn-FYOO-shuh-nihz-uhm)

a belief system that stresses the value of family and the duties that people owe each other

(Lesson 14, page 83)

consumer good (kuhn-SOOM-uhr gud)

a product that people use

(Lesson 7, page 41)

continent (KON-tuh-nuhnt)

one of Earth's seven major landmasses

(Lesson 2, page 10)

Glossary

coral reef (KOR-uhl reef)
an ocean barrier made up
of the hard skeletons of
billions of coral
(*Lesson 15, page 88*)

cultivation (kuhl-tuh-VAY-shuhn)
the act of preparing land and growing crops
(*Lesson 12, page 71*)

cultural diversity
(KUHL-chuhr-uhl duh-VUR-suh-tee)
the state of having people from a variety
of cultures
(*Lesson 3, page 17*)

culture (KUHL-chuhr)
the way of life of a group of people
(*Lesson 3, page 16*)

culture region (KUHL-chuhr REE-juhn)
an area where many people share the same
culture
(*Lesson 3, page 16*)

Dd

deforestation
(dee-fawr-uh-STAY-shuhn)
the cutting down of forests
(*Lesson 5, page 29*)

degree (dih-GREE)
a unit of measure of latitude and longitude;
one 360th of the distance around Earth
(*Lesson 2, page 11*)

delta (DEHL-tuh)
a low, watery land formed by a fan-shaped
system of streams near the mouth of a river
(*Lesson 1, page 5*)

descendant (dih-SEHN-duhnt)
someone related to a person who lived
long ago
(*Lesson 5, page 29*)

desert (DEHZ-uhrt)
a sandy or rocky area
with little or
no rainfall
(*Lesson 8, page 46*)

developing country
(dih-VEHL-uh-pihng KUHN-tree)
a country that is moving from an economy
based on farming to one based on industry
(*Lesson 5, page 29*)

dialect (DY-uh-lehkt)
a different form of the same language
(*Lesson 11, page 65*)

distribution (dihs-truh-BYOO-shuhn)
the spread of something
(*Lesson 14, page 82*)

drought (drowt)
a long time without rain
(*Lesson 9, page 52*)

Ee

earthquake (URTH-kwayk)
a shaking of part of Earth's surface as a result of underground forces
(Lesson 10, page 58)

economy (ih-KON-uh-mee)
a system in which people sell or trade goods and services
(Lesson 3, page 16)

elevation (ehl-uh-VAY-shuhn)
height, as of a mountain
(Lesson 5, page 28)

emigrate (EHM-uh-grayt)
to leave a country in order to live in another
(Lesson 10, page 59)

endangered
(ehn-DAYN-juhrd)
close to disappearing forever because there are so few
(Lesson 9, page 52)

equator (ih-KWAY-tuhr)
an imaginary line around the middle of Earth
(Lesson 2, page 10)

erosion (ih-ROH-zhuhn)
the wearing away of land by water, wind, or ice
(Lesson 10, page 58)

ethnic conflict (EHTH-nihk KON-flihkt)
fighting among ethnic groups
(Lesson 6, page 35)

ethnic group (EHTH-nihk groop)
a group of people who have common ancestors, history, language, and way of life
(Lesson 6, page 35)

European Union
(yur-uh-PEE-uhn YOON-yuhn)
a group of countries in Europe that are working together to make better lives for their people
(Lesson 6, page 35)

export (EHKS-pawrt)
a good that is sold to another country
(Lesson 5, page 29)

Ff

famine (FAM-uhn)
a serious food shortage that causes people to die
(Lesson 9, page 53)

fertile (FUR-tuhl)
able to produce many crops
(Lesson 1, page 5)

fossil fuels (FOS-uhl FYOO-uhlz)
fuels such as coal, oil, and natural gas that formed millions of years ago from the remains of living things
(Lesson 14, page 82)

free trade (free trayd)
the selling of goods from one country to another without taxes
(Lesson 4, page 23)

104

Glossary

frigid (FRIHJ-ihd)
 extremely cold
 (Lesson 15, page 89)

Gg

geography (jee-OG-ruh-fee)
 the study of the earth and the relationship
 between people and the earth
 (Lesson 1, page 4)

global economy (GLOH-buhl ih-KON-uh-mee)
 a world economic system
 (Lesson 13, page 77)

global warming (GLOH-buhl WAWR-mihng)
 the rise in the temperature of Earth's lands
 and oceans
 (Lesson 15, page 89)

gorge (gawrj)
 a canyon with steep walls
 (Lesson 14, page 83)

government (GUHV-uhrn-muhnt)
 a small group of people who make laws to
 rule a large group of people
 (Lesson 3, page 16)

Green Revolution
 (green rehv-uh-LOO-shuhn)
 a movement aimed at improving farming
 methods and crop yields
 (Lesson 11, page 65)

Hh

haiku (HY-koo)
 a traditional Japanese poem written in three
 lines with five, seven, and five syllables.
 (Lesson 13, page 76)

hemisphere (HEHM-uh-sfihr)
 half of Earth
 (Lesson 2, page 10)

Hinduism
 (HIHN-du-ihz-uhm)
 an Indian religion based
 on the belief in many
 gods and reincarnation
 (Lesson 11, page 65)

homogeneous society
 (hoh-muh-JEEN-yuhs suh-SY-uh-tee)
 a society made up of mostly the same kind
 of people
 (Lesson 13, page 76)

human rights (HYOO-muhn ryts)
 rights that every person should have
 (Lesson 14, page 83)

hydroelectricity
 (hy-droh-ih-lehk-TRIHS-uh-tee)
 energy created by water
 falling over a dam
 (Lesson 14, page 83)

ice cap (ys kap)
a thick layer of ice and snow
(Lesson 15, page 89)

illiterate (ih-LIHT-uhr-iht)
unable to read and write
(Lesson 9, page 53)

immigrant (IHM-uh-gruhnt)
someone who comes to another country
to live
(Lesson 4, page 23)

indigenous (ihn-DIHJ-uh-nuhs)
natural or native to a place
(Lesson 15, page 89)

industrialization
(ihn-duhs-tree-uh-luh-ZAY-shuhn)
the making of many goods by machine
(Lesson 3, page 17)

information technology
(ihn-fuhr-MAY-shuhn tehk-NOL-uh-jee)
the use of computer hardware, software,
and the Internet to help people to process
information
(Lesson 11, page 65)

inhabited (ihn-HAB-uh-tihd)
having people living there
(Lesson 12, page 70)

interdependence
(ihn-tuhr-dih-PEHN-duhns)
the state of countries relying on and
affecting each other
(Lesson 13, page 77)

irrigation
(ihr-uh-GAY-shuhn)
the process of bringing
water to dry land
(Lesson 1, page 5)

Islam (ihs-LAHM)
the religion based on the teachings of
Muhammad
(Lesson 8, page 47)

isolation (y-suh-LAY-shuhn)
a state of being cut off from other areas
and people
(Lesson 13, page 76)

kabuki (kah-BOO-kee)
a form of Japanese
drama that combines
singing, dancing, bold
makeup, and elaborate
costumes
(Lesson 13, page 77)

lagoon (luh-GOON)
the shallow ocean
water between a
coral reef and the
shore, or in the
middle of an atoll
(Lesson 15, page 88)

Glossary

landform (LAND-fawrm)
a feature of Earth's surface
(Lesson 1, page 4)

landlocked (LAND-lokt)
surrounded by land
(Lesson 10, page 58)

latitude (LAT-uh-tood)
a series of imaginary lines that
circle Earth from east to west
(Lesson 2, page 11)

life expectancy (lyf ehk-SPEHK-tuhn-see)
how long people are expected to live
(Lesson 9, page 53)

longitude (LON-juh-tood)
a series of imaginary lines that run from the
North Pole to the South Pole
(Lesson 2, page 11)

Mm

manufacturing (man-yuh-FAK-chuhr-ing)
the making of goods by machine
(Lesson 6, page 35)

map key (map kee)
a guide to the lines, colors, and symbols
on a map
(Lesson 2, page 11)

map scale (map skayl)
a comparison between distances shown
on a map to actual distances on Earth
(Lesson 2, page 11)

market economy
(MAHR-kiht ih-KON-uh-mee)
a system in which business owners compete
with one another to sell goods and services
(Lesson 4, page 23)

martial arts (MAHR-shuhl ahrts)
traditional forms of fighting that mainly use
the hands and feet instead of weapons
(Lesson 13, page 77)

migration (my-GRAY-shuhn)
the movement of people from one place to
another
(Lesson 3, page 17)

monsoon (mon-SOON)
a seasonal wind that changes direction
twice a year
(Lesson 11, page 64)

mosque (mosk)
a Muslim building
of worship
(Lesson 8, page 47)

mountain range (MOWN-tuhn raynj)
a long chain of mountains
(Lesson 4, page 22)

Nn

nationalism (NASH-uh-nuh-lihz-uhm)
a strong pride in and loyalty to one's
country
(Lesson 8, page 47)

natural resource
(NACH-uhr-uhl rih-SAWRS)
something in nature that people can use
(Lesson 4, page 22)

nomad (NOH-mad)
a person who travels from
place to place in search of
food or grazing for animals
(Lesson 10, page 59)

Oo _____

oasis (oh-AY-sihs)
an area in the desert that has water
from underground
(Lesson 8, page 46)

outback (OWT-bak)
the dry interior plains
of Australia
(Lesson 15, page 89)

overgrazing (oh-vuhr-GRAY-zihng)
what happens when animals eat grass faster
than it can grow back
(Lesson 8, page 46)

overpopulation
(oh-vuhr-pop-yuh-LAY-shuhn)
the state of having more people in an area
than the resources can support
(Lesson 9, page 53)

Pp _____

paddy (PAD-ee)
a flooded field where rice is grown
(Lesson 12, page 71)

pagoda (puh-GOH-duh)
an Asian tower with
many levels that may
serve as a temple
(Lesson 11, page 65)

peninsula (puh-NIHN-suh-luh)
an area of land that extends from a
landmass and is mostly surrounded by water
(Lesson 6, page 34)

permafrost (PUR-muh-frawst)
an area where the ground is always frozen
a little below the surface
(Lesson 7, page 40)

petroleum (puh-TROH-lee-uhm)
an oily liquid that people burn to create
energy
(Lesson 8, page 47)

plain (playn)
a flat land with few trees, also called
a prairie
(Lesson 4, page 23)

plateau (pla-TOH)
a high, flat landform
(Lesson 5, page 28)

pollution

(puh-LOO-shuhn)
the poisoning
of water, land,
and air
(*Lesson 7, page 41*)

population density

(pop-yuh-LAY-shuhn DEHN-suh-tee)
the average number of people per square
mile living in an area
(*Lesson 3, page 17*)

port (pohrt)

a place where
ships can dock
(*Lesson 12, page
71*)

precipitation (prih-sihp-uh-TAY-shuhn)
water that falls to Earth as rain or snow
(*Lesson 10, page 58*)

privatization (PRY-viht-i-zay-shuhn)
the process of replacing government
ownership of businesses with private
ownership
(*Lesson 7, page 41*)

Rr _____

reincarnation (ree-ihn-kahr-NAY-shuhn)
the idea that each soul must be reborn
many times
(*Lesson 11, page 65*)

relative location

(REHL-uh-tihv loh-KAY-shuhn)
the position of one place in relation to
another place
(*Lesson 2, page 11*)

repression (rih-PREHSH-uhn)
the putting down of citizens' human rights
(*Lesson 14, page 83*)

reservoir (REHZ-uhr-vwahr)
a lake created to store water
(*Lesson 14, page 83*)

rift (rihft)
a broad, steep-walled valley
(*Lesson 9, page 53*)

Ring of Fire (rihng ov fyr)
an area of volcanic activity along
the Pacific Ocean
(*Lesson 12, page 70*)

river system (RIHV-uhr SIHS-tuhm)
a network of streams and rivers that feeds
into a main river
(*Lesson 1, page 5*)

rural (RUR-uhl)
related to open spaces or the countryside
(*Lesson 3, page 17*)

Ss _____

savanna

(suh-VAN-uh)
flat grassland with few
trees and shrubs
(*Lesson 9, page 52*)

service industry (SUR-vihs IHN-duh-stree)
a group of businesses that provides services
(Lesson 6, page 35)

Silk Road (sihlk rohd)
a trade route that went from China, through
Central Asia, to the Mediterranean Sea
(Lesson 10, page 59)

species (SPEE-sheez)
a separate kind of living
thing
(Lesson 15, page 89)

standard of living
(STAN-duhrd ov LIHV-ihng)
a measure of the quality of life. It includes
having good food, housing, education, and
healthcare.
(Lesson 4, page 23)

steppe (stehp)
a dry, flat grassland
(Lesson 7, page 40)

strait (strayt)
a narrow strip of water between large areas
of land
(Lesson 12, page 71)

subcontinent (suhb-KON-tuh-nuhnt)
a large area that is cut off from the rest
of a continent by land features
(Lesson 11, page 64)

subsistence farming
(suhb-SIHS-tuhns FAHR-mihng)
growing only enough crops to provide
for one's basic food needs
(Lesson 9, page 53)

supply and demand
(suh-PLY and dih-MAND)
an economic concept
that states that the price
of a good rises or falls
depending on how many
people want it and on how
much of the good is available
(Lesson 8, page 47)

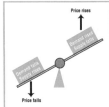

Tt _____

taiga (TY-guh)
an area of evergreen
forests
(Lesson 7, page 40)

Taoism (TOW-ihz-uhm)
a belief system that stresses finding inner
peace and accepting change
(Lesson 14, page 83)

technology (tehk-NOL-uh-jee)
the use of new ideas and machines
to improve people's lives
(Lesson 4, page 23)

terrace farming
(TEHR-ihs FAHR-mihng)
the growing of crops on
step-like levels cut into
the soil
(Lesson 12, page 71)

Glossary

theocracy (thee-OK-ruh-see)
a government ruled by a religious leader
(Lesson 8, page 47)

tourism (TUR-ihz-uhm)
the business of helping people travel
on vacations
(Lesson 6, page 35)

trade deficit (trayd DEHF-uh-siht)
a result of more imports than exports
(Lesson 13, page 77)

trade surplus (trayd SUR-pluhs)
a result of more exports than imports
(Lesson 13, page 77)

tradition (truh-DIHSH-uhn)
a belief or custom handed down from one
generation to the next
(Lesson 10, page 59)

tribe (tryb)
a group of people who share a way of life
(Lesson 10, page 59)

tributary (TRIHB-yuh-tehr-ee)
a stream that joins others and flows
into a river or lake
(Lesson 4, page 22)

tropical climate (TROP-uh-kuhl KLY-miht)
a very warm, moist pattern of weather
(Lesson 5, page 29)

tsunami (tsoo-NAH-mee)
a huge sea wave caused by an underwater
earthquake
(Lesson 12, page 70)

tundra (TUHN-druh)
a flat, bare plain with
no trees
(Lesson 7, page 40)

typhoon (ty-FOON)
a violent storm that occurs in the
Pacific Ocean
(Lesson 12, page 71)

Uu

urban (UR-buhn)
related to the city
(Lesson 3, page 17)

Vv

vegetation (vehj-uh-TAY-shuhn)
the plant life, including trees, bushes,
and grasses in an area
(Lesson 1, page 4)

volcano (vol-KAY-noh)
an opening in Earth's
crust through which
liquid rock and
gases flow
(Lesson 5, page 28)

Acknowledgments

Developer: Maureen Devine Sotoohi
Writer: DeVona Dors
Cover Design: Susan Hawk
Designer: Pat Lucas
Photo Credits:

Cover: clockwise from top left: Wikipedia Commons; ©2007 JupiterImages Corporation; Courtesy of NASA; ©Ludovic Maisant/CORBIS

p. 5   Jonathan Larsen/Shutterstock.com
p. 16   David Ranson/Shutterstock.com
p. 17   (right) ©Jose Fuste Raga/Corbis, (left) Vivian Moos/CORBIS
p. 23   ©Bettmann/CORBIS
p. 29   (left) Salamanderman/Shutterstock.com; (right) ©Collart Herve/CORBIS Sygma
p. 35   (top) Wikipedia Commons; (bottom) Lidian/Shutterstock.com
p. 41   (top) ©Bettmann/CORBIS; (bottom) Courtesy of Oak Ridge National Laboratory
p. 47   (left) ©Iconotec; (right) ©George Steinmetz/CORBIS
p. 53   (top left) Courtesy of NASA; (bottom left) Courtesy of NASA; (right) ©2003 IMS Communications
p. 59   (top) ©Ludovic Maisant/CORBIS; (bottom) ©Unlisted Images, Inc.
p. 65   (left) HIP/Art Resource, NY; (top) Pichogin Dmitry/Shutterstock.com; (bottom) ©Sherwin Crasto/Reuters/Corbis
p. 71   (top) ©2007 JupiterImages Corporation; (bottom) Aiti/Shutterstock.com
p. 77   (top left) ©Dean Conger/CORBIS; (top right) ©Corbis; (bottom right) ©2007 JupiterImages Corporation
p. 83   (top) ©Xiaoyang Liu/Corbis; (bottom) Tamir Niv/Shutterstock.com;
p. 89   (top) Ian Scott/Shutterstock.com; (bottom) Glenn Walker/Shutterstock.com

p. 101 (agriculture) Ivo Vitanov Velinov/Shutterstock.com; (atoll) Albo/Shutterstock.com; (calligraphy) ©Dean Conger/CORBIS
p. 102 (colonization) ©2007 JupiterImages Corporation; (common currency) Ioannis Ionnou/Shutterstock.com
p. 103 (coral reef) Ian Scott/Shutterstock.com; (deforestation) ©Collart Herve/CORBIS Sygma; (desert) Pichugin Dmitry/Shutterstock.com; (drought) Wojciech/Shutterstock.com
p. 104 (endangered) The Final Image/Shutterstock.com; (export) Danesteffes/Shutterstock.com
p. 105 (frigid) Vera Bogaerts/Shutterstock.com; (gorge) Eric Isselee/Shutterstock.com; (Hinduism) HIP/Art Resource, NY; (hydroelectricity) Nancy Brammer/Shutterstock.com
p. 106 (irrigation) Jonathan Larsen/Shutterstock.com; (kabuki) ©Pierre Perrin/Sygma/CORBIS; (lagoon) Digitalife/Shutterstock.com
p. 107 (mosque) ©2007 JupiterImages Corporation
p. 108 (nomad) ©Ludovic Maisant/CORBIS; (outback) Mdd/Shutterstock.com; (pagoda) Tamir Niv/Shutterstock.com
p. 109 (pollution) Courtesy of Oak Ridge National Laboratory; (port) Christopher Penler/Shutterstock.com; (reservoir) Brian C. Lambert/Shutterstock.com; (savanna) Eric Iselee/Shutterstock.com
p. 110 (species) Emin Kuliyev/Shutterstock.com; (steppe) Tropinina Olga/Shutterstock.com; (taiga) Zastavkin/Shutterstock.com; (terrace farming) ©2007 JupiterImages Corporation
p. 111 (tundra) Albert Lozano/Shutterstock.com; (urban) Vivian Moos/CORBIS; (volcano) Inigo Carrera/Shutterstock.com

Illustration Credits:
pp. 4, 10, 11, 22, 23, 28, 34, 40, 46, (bottom) 47, 52, 58, (center) 59, 64, 70, 76, 82, 88, (bottom left) 101, (top right) 110 Pat Lucas
p. 5 Jamie Ruh